GREENER
THAN THOU

Are You *Really* an Environmentalist?

Terry L. Anderson

and

Laura E. Huggins

HOOVER INSTITUTION PRESS

Stanford University   Stanford, California

The Hoover Institution on War, Revolution and Peace, founded at Stanford University in 1919 by Herbert Hoover, who went on to become the thirty-first president of the United States, is an interdisciplinary research center for advanced study on domestic and international affairs. The views expressed in its publications are entirely those of the authors and do not necessarily reflect the views of the staff, officers, or Board of Overseers of the Hoover Institution.

www.hoover.org

Hoover Institution Press Publication No. 559
Hoover Institution at Leland Stanford Junior University,
Stanford, California, 94305-6010

See pages 135–136 for a listing of illustration
sources, credits, and acknowledgements

First printing 2008
15   14   13   12   11   10   09   08   9 8 7 6 5 4 3 2 1

Manufactured in the United States of America

The paper used in this publication meets the minimum
Requirements of the American National Standard for
Information Sciences—Permanence of Paper for Printed
Library Materials, ANSI/NISO Z39.48-1992. ∞

Library of Congress Cataloging-in-Publication Data
Anderson, Terry Lee, 1946–
Greener than thou : are you really an environmentalist? /
by Terry L. Anderson and Laura E. Huggins.
        p.   cm. — (Hoover Institution Press publication ; no. 559)
Includes bibliographical references and index.
ISBN 978-0-8179-4851-1 (hardback : alk. paper) —
ISBN 978-0-8179-4852-8 (pbk. : alk. paper)
1. Environmentalism—United States.   2. Environmentalists—United States.
I. Huggins, Laura E., 1976–   . II. Title.   III. Series: Hoover Institution Press
publication ; 559.
GE197.A66 2008
333.72—dc22   2008013658

Contents

Foreword

The Hoover Institution is designing and implementing task forces on specific topics that coincide with Hoover's ongoing research initiatives. Representing multiyear efforts, the task forces will adopt a methodology whereby a team of experts, both Hoover fellows and other prominent scholars, are brought together and organized as a team, or "virtual faculty," to work on commonly defined topics and projects. One of these new task force efforts, with lead sponsorship by John and Jean DeNault, is the Task Force on Property Rights, Freedom, and Prosperity.

The premise behind Terry Anderson and Laura Huggin's new book, *Greener Than Thou*, complements Hoover's broader effort of understanding the role of property rights in a free society in the above-mentioned task force. In *Greener Than Thou*, Anderson and Huggins address the critical link between property ownership and care for assets, as evidenced in the poignantly titled chapter 4, "No One Washes a Rental Car." Throughout the book, Anderson and Huggins delve deeply into how best to use property rights and markets to convert the environment from a problem into an asset, providing a convincing alternative to regulation via the property rights and market path. Not only do property rights lead to prosperity, which in turn leads to environmental quality, but the combination of property rights and markets makes the environment an asset that can receive careful stewardship from its owner.

In *Greener Than Thou*, Anderson and Huggins take an insightful look into the role of property rights and make a powerful argument for free market environmentalism. Both authors are well suited to address the issues put forward in this book, as evidenced by their previous Hoover Press book, *Property Rights: A Practical Guide to Freedom and Prosperity* (2003), which addressed the complex concepts surrounding the study of property rights.

Terry L. Anderson is the John and Jean DeNault Senior Fellow at the Hoover Institution; the executive director of the Property and Environment Research Center (PERC), a think tank focusing on market solutions to environmental problems located in Montana; and a professor emeritus at Montana State University. Considered the founder of free market environmentalism, he is the author of more than thirty books. Additionally, Anderson has been named codirector of the Task Force on Property Rights, Freedom, and Prosperity.

Laura E. Huggins is a research fellow at the Hoover Institution and director of publications at PERC. She is the author, along with Terry Anderson, of *Property Rights: A Practical Guide to Freedom and Prosperity* (2003). She also edited *Population Puzzle: Boom or Bust?* (2005).

Whether it is stimulating prosperity, making corporations more accountable to their shareholders, encouraging investment in innovation, or improving environmental quality, property rights are essential. By bringing together scholars and policy analysts to study and discuss property rights, the Hoover Institution is positioned to be a leader in the debates about how to encourage freedom and prosperity. The ideas and efforts set forth in *Greener Than Thou* by my colleagues Anderson and Huggins are a critical piece in bringing the issues of property rights to light. This book is a superb accompaniment to Hoover's Task Force on Property Rights, Freedom, and Prosperity and a contribution to the public discourse on the role of property rights and, in many cases, the lack thereof, in recent years.

John Raisian
Tad and Dianne Taube Director
Hoover Institution

Acknowledgments

Greener Than Thou has benefited from discussion, inputs, and comments from various people who are working hard to turn environmental problems into assets. We wish to express our deep appreciation to all of those who helped prepare this monograph, and in particular to Richard Baker, Katy Hansen, and Adam Pope whose research assistance were first-class. Thanks are also due to those who reviewed various chapters including: Rocky Barker, Tim Cranston, Brent Haglund, P. J. Hill, and Robert Nelson. We would also like to recognize Renee Storm whose perseverance in the permissions process was impressive, and of course the Hoover Institution Press, which always go above and beyond to turn straw into gold. Finally and not least, we wish to express warm thanks to John Raisian, director of the Hoover Institution. His vision of the environment goes well beyond the green façade to see that property rights, the rule of law, and limited government provide the foundation for both economic growth and environmental quality to flourish.

1 It's Not Easy Being Green

Kermit the Muppet frog was correct when he croaked, "It's not easy being green." He is lucky he isn't playing in the current environmental arena, where he would find it even harder to be green. Why? Because green is in. It is impossible to read a newspaper or magazine, turn on the radio or television, or engage in a cocktail party conversation without the words "green" or "eco" popping up. There are green television stations, green termite killers, green cars, eco-moms, eco-fashion, eco-tours, and the list goes on. Everyone insists on being *Greener Than Thou.*

Politicians, big business, and even religious groups are also vying for the green spotlight. Whoever can out green the other gets to set the regulation, and if you don't jump on the bandwagon you risk being left behind altogether. The race to apply red tape to green problems is being disguised as a duty of moral leadership. In terms of real environmental improvements, however, this greener-than-thou attitude is dangerous. Beware of those jockeying to make Kermit pale by comparison.

Politicians, even the red (Republican) ones, cannot resist the green glamour. Consider President George W. Bush's stance on global warming. When Bush announced his candidacy, he questioned whether global warming was real. At the nadir of his presidency, he added polar bears to the endangered species list, blaming the listing on global warming and advocated a limited cap-and-trade program for greenhouse gas emissions—a full reversal of his original position.

Or what about the Republican Arnold Schwarzenegger, whom *The*

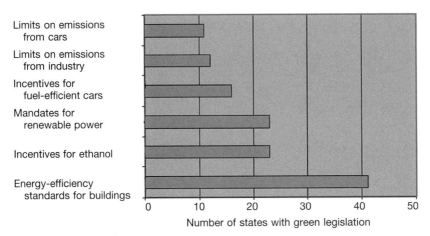

Figure 1. Green Legislation
Many states created laws or incentives to promote green legislation and thus
compete to be green. The competition is especially stiff in the areas of ethanol and
energy-efficiency standards for buildings.
Source: "Green America: Waking Up and Catching Up," *The Economist*, January 25,
2007, pp. 22–24.

Economist called "the decidedly green governor of California" (Green
America 2007, 23). In his bid to be greener-than-thou, he required
California utilities to reduce carbon dioxide emissions by 10 percent
by 2020, pushed for state mandates for increased automobile fuel efficiency, and allowed the state to sue car manufacturers for damages
due to global warming and to sue the Environmental Protection
Agency for not regulating greenhouse gas emissions.

Although California has adopted the most comprehensive legislation, other states are not far behind (see figure 1). More than 300
bills related to climate change were introduced in forty states (Cizik
2007). And the Western Governors Association voted unanimously to
approve the Clean and Diversified Energy Initiative—75 percent of
the governors represented red states.

On many political issues Democrats and Republicans take opposite sides of the debate. On minimum-wage legislation, for example,
Democrats push for higher wages to help improve the living standards

of low-paid workers, whereas Republicans try to keep wages down on the theory that higher wages eliminate jobs. On taxes, Democrats call for lower taxes on the poor because they are less able to pay; Republicans call for lower taxes on the rich in an effort to encourage investment and productivity.

When it comes to the environment, however, both battle for the regulatory high ground. Regardless of political colors, it seems that being green equates to top-down control. Democrats criticize the environmental record of the Bush administration and recall the good ole final days of the Clinton administration when strict standards were placed on arsenic levels in streams and lakes and when millions of acres were declared roadless. And they embrace Al Gore's sermons on Capitol Hill calling for fast track regulations to curb global warming.

Republicans yearn for days even farther back in their history. They cling to the claim that Theodore Roosevelt was the original conservative conservationist, despite the fact that he greatly expanded ownership of federal land, which entrenched resource socialism on the U.S. landscape. They also point out that Richard Nixon was the first environmental president because he signed several environmental acts, including the Clean Air Act, and instituted the Environmental Protection Agency—one of the biggest and fastest-growing regulatory agencies in Washington. Although those green policies have led to some improvements, they come wrapped in red tape that has been expensive and created gridlock.

Support for environmental regulation is also growing among some unlikely groups such as evangelicals. Protection of the environment, they say, is a biblically rooted commandment, causing many religious groups to see global warming as a moral issue and thus being greener than thou as a must. As Richard Cizik with the National Association of Evangelicals stated, we should see the global warming crisis as "a note from God that says, 'I said to be a good steward, my children. Sin has consequence, and if you pollute the earth there will be a price to pay'" (Cizik 2007, 92). The Evangelical Climate Initiative encour-

aged pastors to sign a "Call to Action," and the Evangelical Environmental Network's website asks, "What would Jesus drive?" The combination of holier than thou with greener than thou has only strengthened regulatory environmentalism.

Even big business, although risking being strangled by environmental restrictions, is accepting that change is in the air. For example, four-fifths of utility executives polled by Cambridge Energy Research Associates expect mandatory emission caps within ten years ("Green America 2007"). If regulation is on its way, then companies that help define the rules have a better chance of winning the game. At the very least, businesses want to avoid a patchwork of conflicting local environmental regulations, a scenario that is already causing confusion as states such as California are setting stricter standards than the federal government. Moreover, many firms who caught the green wave early have been able to make some green out of green. General Electric and Goldman Sachs, for example, actively support going green—because they think there is money to be made and more influence to be had over policymakers.

"It's always cozy in here. We're insulated by layers of bureaucracy."

So why is green equated with regulation and not with harnessing the power of markets to improve the environment? Is there another path to better resource stewardship? Is it possible to be a free market environmentalist?

Free Market Environmentalism

Traditional thinking about environmental issues has tended to emphasize incentive problems inherent in markets but ignore them in the context of political processes. Many policymakers assume that an efficient allocation of resources will be reached when government correctly accounts for all the costs and benefits.

"I do know one thing, gentlemen. If we don't plug into the environment right now, we're going to be missing out on a lot of big envirobucks."

The call for a carbon tax is a classic example. When a person or business decides to consume fossil fuels, carbon dioxide is emitted into the atmosphere. Because fossil fuel consumers do not take into account the cost of extra carbon emissions on others, the energy market is seen as failing. To correct this alleged failure, the government attempts to determine the costs being imposed on others and impose a tax on emissions to account for those costs. Thus, a carbon tax increases the cost of fossil fuel, inducing the consumer to use less, with the presumption that government regulation is necessary to reach some hypothetically optimal level of fossil fuel consumption.

Free market environmentalism (FME) challenges the assumption that the policymaker has sufficient knowledge to set the optimal tax. Knowing the optimal level of emissions and the optimal tax rate is not, in the words of Nobel laureate Friedrich Hayek, "given to any one mind." The policymaker needs information about production processes, production costs, and the health and consumption effects of the product. No one person or group of people, however well informed, can determine the optimal emissions or tax through a centralized process. The best mechanism we have for discovering the optimal emissions is through a decentralized process that can aggregate diffuse knowledge; this process is a market.

Free market environmentalism emphasizes the important role of markets, incentives, and property rights. At the heart of FME is a system of property rights to natural resources that, whether held by individuals or a group, create inherent incentives for resource users because the wealth of the owner is at stake if bad decisions are made. In short, free market environmentalists strive to transform environmental problems into assets.

FME was pioneered in the early 1980s and laid out in detail in the book by that title, *Free Market Environmentalism* (Anderson and Leal 1991; Anderson and Leal 2001). Because the ideas were controversial at the time, a reviewer called the title an oxymoron, probably because people often assume free markets mean that corporations can do whatever they please, including polluting the air and water without concern for the consequences. In such a system, landowners will overcut their trees, overplow their soil, and overgraze their pastures. How, then, can markets solve the problems they are seen as causing?

To help answer the question, let us first examine four environmental so-called truisms that plague market approaches, keeping in mind that free market environmentalists try to see the world the way it is, not the way it ought be. It is fine to wish for better stewardship and environmental quality, but ultimately good policy must focus on what really works. Understanding the fallacies behind these environmental truisms helps illuminate another path to environmental quality.

1. Environmental quality, priceless

Every transaction involves a trade-off, something that must be given up to get what we want. There is only so much land, so if we "put in a parking lot," as Joni Mitchell put it in her 1975 hit song "Big Yellow Taxi," we will have to "pave paradise," thus sacrificing farm-land, open space, or wildlife habitat. But the opposite is also true: if we don't pave paradise, we won't have the hospital, supermarket, or school—all of which add value to our lives. If we conserve energy, we live in cooler houses in the winter and warmer ones in the summer, we drive fewer miles, and we drive smaller cars. If we recycle, we devote time to sorting our garbage, live with the inconvenience of recycling bins, and drive or walk out of our way to the recycling center. If you are green, you are expected to oppose paving paradise and to favor conserving energy and recycling regardless of the cost. Such axiomatic rules, however, ignore the trade-offs inherent in all transactions.

We see the same problem in debates over how to confront green-house gas emissions and global warming. Despite there being no sci-entific models to suggest that proposed global warming policies will significantly reduce the effect of climate change, people continue to call for action. The pragmatist asks, what are the costs of this action? The seven-hundred-page Stern Report (2006) commissioned by the British government estimates that the costs of stabilizing greenhouse gas concentrations to be approximately 1 percent of global output per year and possibly higher. The report also contends that the cost of not stabilizing greenhouse gases could be between 5 percent and 20 percent of global output per year (see chapter 3 for a more detailed discussion).

Serious economists have little good to say about these estimates, for two reasons. First, the costs of doing nothing are unlikely to prevail because we will almost certainly find cheaper ways than we have now to reduce carbon consumption. As just one example, ponder the re-birth of the nuclear power industry in the United States; part of that renaissance is owed to the concern over coal-fired power plants.

Second, the costs will have to be incurred now and the benefits, if any, will surface far into the future (Becker 2007). None of us are willing to take on significant costs today without some possibility of a return on our investment. So why invest trillions of dollars now to reduce carbon if we cannot expect a return in the next hundred years? Even the most liberal policy analyst must wonder whether emission-reduction policies make good economic sense. Free market environmentalists recognize that improving environmental quality comes at a cost and that these costs must be weighed against the benefits.

2. Mother nature and materialism don't mix

Because free enterprise leads to higher incomes and higher incomes lead to greater ability to consume, it is easy to see why free market ideas might be seen as promoting materialism. But as people in developing countries move beyond meeting their basic needs of food, clothing, and shelter, they begin wanting cell phones, televisions, and cars.

Of course, human welfare goes far beyond meeting material wants and needs to include health and happiness. As the late policy analyst Aaron Wildovsky liked to put it, "wealthier is healthier." On this narrow dimension, the wealth that comes with higher incomes allows people to enjoy better nutrition, improved health, longer lives, and cleaner environments (see figure 2).

An important relationship exists between wealth and environmental quality. In the early stages of economic development, people often are willing to sacrifice environmental quality for higher incomes; water and air quality may deteriorate and resources may be exploited to increase incomes. But as wealth rises and people move beyond

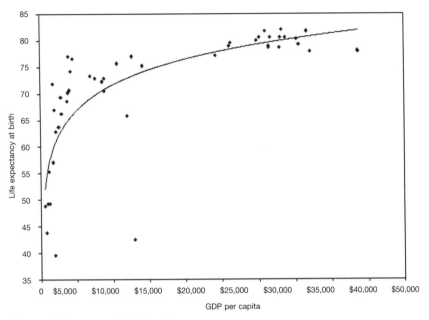

Figure 2. Poverty and Life Expectancy
As GDP increases, life expectancy does as well. The figure shows data for 48
countries, with incomes as high as $43,500 in Switzerland and as low as $600 in
Somalia. The average life expectancy ranges from 39.5 years in Zimbabwe to 82
years in Japan. Countries such as the United States and Sweden have high incomes
and a high average life expectancy. South Africa, Afghanistan, and Kenya have low
incomes and a low average life expectancy.
Source: The World Factbook. 2007. Central Intelligence Agency. Available online at
www.cia.gov/library/publications/the-world-factbook/ (accessed June 20, 2007).

subsistence, they begin to demand better stewardship and environmental quality (see chapter 3).

As the U.S. founding fathers understood, the right to pursue life,
liberty, and happiness is fundamental and best met through free enterprise and private ownership. If free people choose materialism, especially as they emerge from poverty, so be it. Some might think that
even those at low-income levels ought to choose spiritual, cultural, or
environmental fulfillment, but freedom means accepting a person's
choice to buy an iPod rather than protect endangered species. The

data show that wealth ultimately leads to better health and environmental quality.

3. Markets know no limits

Free enterprise cannot exist without secure private property rights, but those rights do not mean that the owner can do whatever he or she pleases. Property rights allow the owner to reap the benefits of ownership but also to be held responsible for how the property is used.

Property rights must be clearly defined, enforced, and transferable on a willing buyer–willing seller basis. When all those conditions are present, the owner is then able to decide how and by whom the property will be used. Definition and enforcement also mean that others cannot trespass. Hence, far from allowing people in a free society to do whatever they please, private ownership requires that people take only actions that do not harm others (Anderson and Huggins 2003).

In the context of environmentalism, secure property rights can help keep waste contained. For example, if a person throws garbage into a neighbor's backyard, the neighbor will have recourse against the dumper because the property rights are clear: the backyard belongs to the neighbor and the garbage belongs to the polluter. It is not always easy, however, to detect who is doing the dumping or who owns the backyard: Case in point, if the garbage is dumped into a river that is unowned and mixes together, it can be difficult to determine who is doing the dumping and difficult to assign responsibility.

This, however, is what courts are in the business of resolving. Consider the case of *Jacobs Farms, Inc. v. Western Farm Services.* In a coastal city in central California, Western Farm Services legally applied pesticides to a conventional farm; fog turned the pesticide to liquid droplets and air currents carried them to the organic Jacobs Farms, destroying $500,000 worth of dill. Under state law, the sprayer's responsibility ends once the chemicals have been applied; Western Farm

Services thus did not violate the law. Attorneys representing Jacobs Farms, however, argued that neighboring farms were responsible for the pesticide that contaminated the organic crops, convincing a Santa Cruz County Superior Court judge to order Western Farm Services to stop spraying pesticides (Bookwalter 2007).

For free market environmentalists, one of government's most important roles is to define and enforce property rights, thus encouraging environmental stewardship. Water rights in the American West provide a good example. In the early days of mining camps and farming communities, people claimed water by diverting it for beneficial uses, basing their claims on who had diverted the water first. Associations such as irrigation districts were formed to monitor water use. Known as the prior appropriation system, those well-defined and enforced water rights created the basis for trade and reallocation of water from lower-valued to higher-valued uses. Thus, the farmer wanting to increase irrigated acreage in a valuable crop such as grapes can purchase water from farmers with low-valued crops such as hay. Growing cities can purchase water from farmers to quench their thirst. Such exchanges encourage water conservation if the conserved water can be sold in the marketplace.

Unfortunately, proof of beneficial use required diversion and did not count water left in streams as a beneficial use. If water for fish and wildlife habitat and pollution dilution is valued more than water for agricultural, municipal, or industrial uses, those seeking additional water cannot purchase diversion rights and leave the extra water in the stream. Moreover, the irrigator who cannot sell her water to trout fishers for fish habitat has no incentive to worry about the value of water for instream uses; if she can sell and chooses not to do so, she bears the cost of saying no and thus has an incentive to at least consider purchase offers.

Fortunately, as we will see in chapter 5, growing demands for environmental water uses have pressured state legislatures to change the rules. As a result, in states such as Oregon, Montana, and Colo-

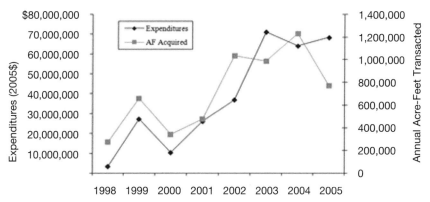

Figure 3. Acquisitions of Water (1998–2005)
In most western states, markets for instream flow water rights have grown. The figure shows total expenditures and the quantity of water acquired for instream flows in ten western states: Washington, Oregon, California, Arizona, New Mexico, Colorado, Nevada, Utah, Idaho, and Montana.
Source: Brandon Scarborough and Hertha L. Lund. *Saving Our Streams: Harnessing Water Markets.* (Bozeman, MT: Property and Environment Research Center [PERC], 2007).

rado, environmentalists are using water markets to increase instream flows. The Oregon Water Trust, for example, offers to replace ranchers forgone hay crops if they will leave their irrigation water instream for salmon and steelhead. Such win-win trades have encouraged similar organizations to form in Montana and Washington and spurred an exponential increase in the environmental water market (see figure 3).

4. Don't worry, be happy

In response to concerns from doomsayers that population growth was our greatest environmental problem, the late Julian Simon, a professor of business administration at the University of Maryland, was fond of saying, "With every mouth comes two hands and a mind" and that human ingenuity is "the ultimate resource."

Professor Simon's position was not based on a simple faith in human ingenuity but on evidence. If property rights to natural resources, physical capital, and intellectual capital (human ingenuity) are secure and tradable as described above, people will respond to scarcity by investing in technologies that allow us to better cope.

Confident that these incentives were in place, Simon challenged Paul Ehrlich, the Bing Professor of Population Studies at Stanford and author of the *Population Bomb* (1968), to a bet. Simon, hypothesizing that growing scarcity should result in higher resource prices, bet Ehrlich that such prices would not materialize because of human ingenuity. Ehrlich accepted the wager and was allowed to choose five natural resources that he thought would rise in value between 1980 and 1990. On the basis of $1,000 divided equally among the five metals that he chose, Simon agreed to pay Ehrlich the difference between $1,000 and the price to which the hypothetical bundle rose, and Ehrlich agreed to pay the difference between $1,000 and the price to which it fell (both adjusted for inflation). At the end of the period, not only had the value of the bundle fallen in nominal terms but it had fallen in real terms. Ehrlich mailed Simon a check for $576.07. Simon, confident in the powerful influence of incentives, suggested that they bet again and up the ante to $10,000; Ehrlich declined.

David McClintick and Ross B. Emmett (2005) take the Simon-Ehrlich bet one step further by tracking a composite index of the prices of Ehrlich's five metals from 1900 to 2000. Their finding was that the index was approximately 50 percent lower at the end of the century than at the beginning. They also found, however, that the index was, as Simon suspected, highly volatile. Both of Simon's hypotheses were confirmed: (1) that human ingenuity can overcome the effects of increasing demand and (2) that ingenuity will take time to manifest itself (see chapter 3, figure 5, page 37).

Free market environmentalists are optimistic about human ingenuity and the environment because history shows that resourcefulness leads to positive results. Environmental conditions are improving by almost any measure in areas where incomes are high and growing (the focus of chapter 3). In the United States, for example, air and water quality have improved dramatically from sea to sea. "Don't waste energy worrying about the wrong issue" is a better motto than "Don't worry, be happy." Rather than worrying about the fossil fuel depletion crisis, for example, why not focus on how to use energy more efficiently and on how to create alternative fuel sources.

A Green Thumb for the Invisible Hand

The notion of the power of the "invisible hand," a metaphor for free enterprise, has traveled a long way from its roots in Adam Smith's *The Wealth of Nations* (1776). Today's global marketplace has lifted millions of people out of poverty and has the potential to continue doing so. It has the same potential for improving environmental quality, but most policymakers see markets and globalization as the cause of environmental degradation.

Combating the tendency to equate being green with environmental red tape requires rethinking the role of markets in providing environmental quality. Whether the issue is management of public lands, water or air quality, or global warming, free market environmentalism can provide an alternative to command-and-control regulation.

In what follows, we suggest ways in which FME can do that. The first step is to recognize what Aldo Leopold, the father of modern conservation, realized, namely, that incentives matter. As he put it, "conservation will ultimately boil down to rewarding the private landowner who conserves the public interest" (Leopold 1934, 202). With this in mind, we will show how incentives are leading to environmental improvements. When one considers the evidence, "you have to admit it's [the environment] getting better," as the Beatles' song put it. Just as "no one washes a rental car," people do not take care of natural resources they don't own. If property rights can be established, numerous examples show that "markets are a frog's best friend." By forming local coalitions around market principles, liberals and conservatives can find ways of "dancing with environmentalists" and discover pragmatic solutions that improve environmental quality without increasing regulation.

 It's Aldo,
Not Teddy

We Americans have had a complex relationship with nature. On the one hand, we have exploited the nation's natural resources by clearing forests, damming rivers, and plowing the prairies. On the other hand, we have had philosophers, conservationists, and politicians from Henry David Thoreau to John Muir to Aldo Leopold to Theodore Roosevelt who have raised our environmental consciousness. The result has been not only a tension between the merits of economic growth versus environmental quality, a topic for chapter 3, but also a debate over which of these environmental leaders has offered the best ideas for resolving such tensions.

Conservative environmentalists in particular have had to overcome a reputation for putting growth before environmental stewardship and for lacking a leader who embodies conservative thinking. As author Jeremy Beer (2003) explains, "You might not know it from the exhibit tables at most conservative gatherings, stacked as they are with explicitly anti-environmental flyers, articles, and books, but America's conservative movement was once intimately linked with conservation." This chapter explores the philosophical foundations for free market environmentalism and conservation.

Many conservatives are quick to declare President Theodore Roosevelt the godfather of conservation, often mistakenly claiming that he established Yellowstone National Park. Although Yellowstone was established in 1872, long before his presidency, Roosevelt did focus the nation's attention on the value of the West's natural resources by expanding the national park system and establishing the U.S. Forest

Service to manage millions of acres of public land withdrawn from private claims. Far from creating a philosophical base for conservative conservation, however, his action firmly ensconced natural resource socialism as a mainstay of environmental management.

More recently, President Richard Nixon has been held up as an example of a Republican president who, due to popular demand, became a conservationist. Nixon created the Environmental Protection Agency and signed laws including the Clean Air Act, the Clean Water Act, the Marine Mammal Protection Act, and the National Environmental Policy Act—some of the nation's best examples of command-and-control environmentalism.

Environmentalists claim Aldo Leopold as the icon of modern conservation because he called for a heightened environmental consciousness in the form of a "land ethic" to encourage resource stewardship. According to Leopold, if people would learn to "think like a mountain," they would better understand the complexity of environmental systems and could better conserve them. Of course, because it is difficult to develop such a heightened consciousness, most environmentalists call for interim command-and-control policies to force said consciousness. Hence, Leopold's land ethic inadvertently became the basis for environmental regulation. Yet, returning to his essay "Thinking Like a Mountain," he says, "I have lived to see state after state extirpate its wolves" (Leopold 1966, 130), an explicit, thoughtful condemnation of command-and-control wildlife management.[1] Leopold (1945) knew that wolf extirpation was wildlife execution by government. As we shall see, Leopold, who understood the importance of incentives and the role of the private property owner, might be thought of as the first free market environmentalist.

To understand the philosophical foundations of free market environmentalism, one must look back to the late nineteenth and early

1. Statement based on interview with Brent Haglund, president of the Sand County Foundation (June 8, 2007). See also Leopold 1945, "Review of the Wolves of North America."

twentieth centuries to see the first true push for environmental preservation in the United States. The end of the nineteenth century marked the closing of the frontier, the near extinction of the buffalo, and the disappearance of the passenger pigeon. Land stretching from sea to sea and wildlife numbers in the millions symbolized America's abundant natural resources. Not surprisingly, the end of the frontier and the wholesale reduction of wildlife and its habitat forced people to question nature's boundlessness. Moreover, the Industrial Revolution and the tremendous economic progress it afforded caused people to wonder whether the nation would run out of natural resources. During this same period, economic growth provided people the time and money to demand more environmental amenities such as clean water as well as more commodities such as lumber. Both the concern over scarce resources and the demand for amenities, especially from western lands, manifested themselves in more governmental regulation in the name of conservation.

King Teddy's Bequest

President Theodore Roosevelt (1901–9) is often hailed by environmentalists and conservatives alike as a godfather of conservation. A rancher, big-game hunter, amateur entomologist, and graduate of Harvard, Roosevelt came to the presidency both well schooled and disposed to protect the natural heritage of the nation. He advocated sustainable use of the nation's natural resources, public protection and management of wild game, and the preservation of open spaces. Roosevelt made conservation a central policy issue of his administration, creating national parks, wildlife and bird refuges, the U.S. Forest Service, and the Bureau of Reclamation. He also appointed an Inland Waterways Commission to investigate the condition of the nation's navigable waterways and to recommend measures for their protection and improvement. And, in 1908, he called on state governors to attend the White House Conference on Conservation, now regarded as the official commencement of the national conservation crusade.

Perhaps the greatest legacy of Roosevelt's conservation was his creation of federal management regimes for the nation's natural resources. Resources were to be governed by new land management agencies such as the Forest Service and the Bureau of Reclamation on behalf of the public to achieve the impossible goal of producing "the greatest good for the greatest number."

Roosevelt used this ideological framework in conjunction with the "bully pulpit" of his office to promote his progressive platform. Progressives argued that the economy, society, and government were riddled with inefficiency and that centralized control by experts could identify and fix the problems. Roosevelt and other progressive conservationists such as Gifford Pinchot, the first chief of the U.S. Forest Service, believed that scientifically managing natural resources would enable experts to manage for the masses.

Under this new philosophy, Roosevelt extended the powers of government in general and the executive branch in particular, departing from the laissez-faire policies that underpinned what James Willard Hurst (1956) called "the release of energy" in the nineteenth century. Under the banner of scientific management, much of the West's public land was put under the control of Washington politicians, subordinating local communities and business interests to the federal bureaucracy. During his presidency, Roosevelt set aside 194 million acres (the size of Texas and Louisiana combined).

Federal management is often equated with democratic management, but the latter does not necessarily follow the former. Indeed, naturalist John Muir, patron saint of the Sierra Club and friend of Roosevelt, viewed progressivism as a negative because, in his words, the "greatest number is too often found to be number one" (quoted in Morris 2001, 231).

John Reiger, author of *American Sportsmen and the Origins of Conservation* (2001), points out that people simply accepted the progressive political rhetoric of the early conservation movement as a democratic movement to manage resources for the people instead of for

"I Rather Like That Imported Affair."

industrial special interests. Yet conservation began as an effort of the upper class, raising the question of how could conservation be seen as a democratic movement of the people against the elites when the elites started it.

Historian Samuel P. Hays argued that the goals of progressive conservationists often clashed with grass-roots democratic impulses because the majority of people preferred using traditional resources as commodities rather than amenities. Western water users, for example, fearing their established claims would be threatened under Roosevelt's bureaucratic approach, preferred to present their cases to courts "rather than to permit an administrative determination of rights" that might not be based on the "merits of each individual claim" (Hays 1959, 273). The belief that the federal government was waging war on its citizens was evident in many western papers of the time. The *Steamboat Pilot* (Steamboat Springs, Colo.), for example, trumpeted, "Very few of the autocratic monarchs of the world would so dare to set aside the will of the people this way" (quoted in Miller 2001, 164). Another Colorado newspaper lambasted Roosevelt's conservation efforts as "Russian policy," which was nothing more than "arbitrary and authoritarian rule on the range" (Miller 2001, 164).

Critiques of Roosevelt's environmental leadership raised several viable questions regarding the true spirit of Roosevelt-style conservation. As stated in *Conservation and the Gospel of Efficiency* (Hays 1959, 275–76):

> The first American conservation movement experimented with the application of the new technology to resource management. Requiring centralized and coordinated decisions, however, this procedure conflicted with American political institutions which drew their vitality from filling local needs. This conflict between the centralizing tendencies of effective economic organization and the decentralizing forces inherent in a multitude of geographical interests presented problems to challenge even the wisest statesman. The Theodore Roosevelt administration, essentially hostile to the wide distribution of decision-making, grappled with this problem but failed to solve it. Instead of recognizing the paradoxes, which their own approach raised, conservationists choose merely to identify their opposition as "selfish interests." Yet the conservation movement raised a fundamental question in American life: How can large-scale economic development be effective and at the same time fulfill the desire for significant grass-roots participation?

Roosevelt's Heir

Expanding on the tradition of progressive-era preservationists, President Richard Nixon (1969–74) outmaneuvered Democrats to become Roosevelt's heir. Until the 1968 campaign, the environment had not been an issue for Nixon; he was much more comfortable in matters relating to foreign policy. But Nixon was pushed by public opinion to enter the environmental arena. Consider, for example, that an estimated 20 million people participated in the first Earth Day, April

22, 1970—a day representing the emergence of a new environmentalism. These new environmentalists viewed humanity as a threat to the health of the earth and therefore demanded much broader protection for overall environmental quality (Flippen 2000). Nixon, a canny politician, recognized early on that by committing his administration to regulate the environment he could become greener than thou and gain political currency in the process.

Given the political upheaval surrounding Nixon's tenure in the White House, it is easy to overlook his impact on the emerging environmental movement in America. Nixon, in fact, helped build an unprecedented bureaucratic morass, including the National Environmental Policy Act (NEPA), the Clean Air and Clean Water Acts, the Environmental Protection Agency (EPA), and the Endangered Species Act. As he jockeyed for advantage on regulatory legislation, he also signed into law regulations designed to curb pesticide pollution, regulate ocean dumping, and protect coastal zones and marine animals.

Little noticed when passed by Congress in 1969 and signed by Nixon in 1970, NEPA, often referred to as the environmental Magna Carta, has turned out to be the most influential of the many environmental laws enacted in the 1960s and 1970s. The act's requirement that federal agencies prepare environmental impact statements before taking major action transformed government decision making and became a powerful tool for environmentalists to halt, delay, or modify projects they considered harmful.

The problem is that this tool thwarts efficient management. The average length of an environmental impact statement (EIS), for example, is 570 pages (Black 2004). Moreover, once an EIS is created, it can take years to review it. According to Jim Matson with the Forest Resource Council, "NEPA has evolved into a logjam of overwhelming scale and proportions" (quoted in Coulter 2005).

Others point to the prolonged disputes and the wide range of lawsuits over EISs as hampering NEPA's effectiveness. Abigail Kimbell, chief of the Forest Service, spoke at a congressional hearing, testifying,

*"It's from the government—we'll have to file an
environmental-impact statement before we can evolve."*

"We have 44 projects in some stage of litigation right now. . . . Each time we go through the appeal process or the courts, much of our limited resources are employed to defend the decisions we feel are crucial to restoring ecosystems and addressing forest health concerns" (quoted in Coulter 2005). NEPA lawsuits have been expanded far beyond what Nixon anticipated. For example, in *The Center for Biological Diversity v. United States Department of Housing and Urban Development*, environmental groups sued U.S. authorities for not completing a NEPA analysis before issuing each and every mortgage insurance and loan guarantee (Center for Biological Diversity 2005).

Perhaps NEPA's biggest problem is that it further transformed the environmental landscape away from local management. Under NEPA, outside groups who are not directly affected by a proposed project are often accorded more importance than local interests. The Center for Environmental Quality's review of NEPA (2002) points out that, in many cases, the process is hijacked by well-financed professionals, such as the Sierra Club, who have NEPA specialists standing by to tackle various local issues. And in some cases locals do not find out about an issue in time to offer input.

The inefficiencies of Nixon's environmental policies can also be seen in the Clean Air Act Extension of 1970. An amendment of the weaker and less comprehensive 1963 act, the extension requires the EPA to establish regulations to protect the public from hazardous airborne contaminants. Those regulations were created to reduce intrastate pollution but in many cases produced perverse incentives. For example, states approved industrial plants plans to build taller smokestacks that sent pollution over state boundaries instead of reducing or eliminating pollution.[2]

The extension is hundreds of pages long, and the EPA has written thousands of pages of regulations to comply with its requirements. In the words of environmental policy analyst Joel Schwartz, "EPA regulations and guidance have created a compulsively detailed administrative system that places process and centralized power ahead of results and devotes great resources toward small, expensive, and ineffective pollution reduction measures, while ignoring opportunities for large, cheap, and rapid improvements" (quoted in Lieberman, 2004).

The benefits of complying with Nixon-era regulations are outweighed by the tremendous costs. According to David Schoenbrod, professor of law at New York Law School, "The best estimates are that we could have achieved the present level of environmental quality at a quarter of the direct cost. . . . [T]he current regime of pollution control also creates immense indirect costs, by imposing paper work requirements and by discouraging new plants and innovations" (2000).

Although Roosevelt's and Nixon's intentions may have been good,

---

2. For more information, see "Environmental Federalism: Thinking Smaller," 1996, by Terry L. Anderson and Peter J. Hill.

"Can't we just dye the smoke green?"

those early conservation seeds have grown into our current environmental leviathan. Beginning with Roosevelt's presidency and escalating in the 1970s, environmental policy has focused on top-down governmental regulations to solve environmental problems, with little attention to the knowledge and skills of local resource users. As Leopold asked, "At what point will governmental conservation, like the mastodon, become handicapped by its own dimensions?" (1966, 250).

Aldo Knows Best

One of the first to raise concerns over natural resource socialism was Aldo Leopold. In "The Round River" (1966), pointing out what he claimed to be the root problem with progressive conservation, Leopold used the metaphor of government as a meadowlark. Leopold's bird dog, Gus, when he couldn't find pheasants, became excited about meadowlarks. This "whipped-up zeal for unsatisfactory substitutes masked the dog's failure to find the real thing" (186), temporarily calming the dog's inner frustration. Leopold explained that he did not know which dog in the field caught the first scent of the meadowlark, but he did know that every dog performed an enthusiastic backing-point. The meadowlark symbolized "the idea that if the private land-owner won't practice conservation, let's build a bureau to do it for him" (186). Like the meadowlark, explains Leopold, this substitute has its good points and often smells like success. The trouble is "it contains no device for preventing good private land from becoming poor public land. There is trouble in the assuagement of honest frustration; it helps us forget we have not yet found a pheasant." He concluded by cautioning the reader to be leery of the belief that "whatever ails the land, the government will fix it" (187).

Leopold was an employee of the U.S. Forest Service, a professor of game management at the University of Wisconsin, and a lifelong hunter. Considered by many as the father of wilderness conservation, he studied at the Yale University School of Forestry, which was established by Gifford Pinchot—Roosevelt's first chief of the Forest Service. Leopold initially fell in line with other progressive conservationists but eventually moved beyond this label after his work as a government employee left him with few illusions regarding the limitations of the political process. Leopold came to realize that true environmental protection would be organized around "a conviction of individual responsibility for the health of the land" (quoted in Meine and Knight, 312–13). He believed that those who owned the land were the best stewards because they understood the land's complexity.

Leopold grew up in Burlington, Iowa, at the turn of the twentieth century, in a culture where private land ownership, free enterprise, and individualism were prized (Freyfogle 1999). His character was shaped around these institutions and values, which remained with him throughout his life. Toward the end of his career, he focused on the ethical obligations of the private owner, yet even as he submitted his land ethic to the public, he wore the hat of the private property owner planting trees at his "shack" in Wisconsin. Leopold, according to environmental scholar Eric Freyfogle (1999, 155), "spoke to no audience more directly than the dispersed and powerful owners of private land."

Leopold's realization of the importance of private landowners as stewards and the difficulty of creating a land ethic in governmental bureaucracies paralleled changes in his career and world events. A 1923 article entitled "A Criticism of the Booster Spirit" was a response to Leopold's stint as secretary of the Albuquerque Chamber of Commerce, in which Leopold harped on the narrow values of rapid growth and quick profits that substituted for the sustainable use of local resources and local culture (Flader and Callicott 1991).

In 1924 Leopold left the Forest Service for four years as an administrator at the "hopelessly utilitarian" Forest Products Laboratory in Madison, Wisconsin (quoted in Flader and Callicott 1991). Searching for ways to make his laboratory research relevant to the public, he wrote "The Home Builder Conserves" (1928), an article filled with efforts that private homeowners could take to conserve wood and reduce unnecessary waste. He resigned in 1928 to concentrate on forestry and game management and, in 1933, joined the faculty of the Department of Agricultural Economics at the University of Wisconsin, where he studied broad social and institutional issues.

There, during the depth of the Great Depression, Leopold increasingly emphasized the importance of personal stewardship of the private landowner. In a major address, "Conservation Economics" (1934), Leopold critiqued the effectiveness of conservation through public ownership and governmental agencies. He described conservation "experts" as working at cross-purposes and suggested that economic incentives might be used to reward good stewardship by private individuals. Moreover, he claimed that "exclusively governmental conservation is undemocratic in [the] sense that it declines to credit the private citizen with brains, enthusiasm, or public spirit" (Meine and Knight, 162). Finally, in "Land Pathology," a speech delivered on April 15, 1935, the day after Black Sunday (a devastating dust storm that turned the sky black), Leopold, pointing out that government ownership is remedial rather than preventive, pleaded "for positive and substantial public encouragement, economic and moral, for the land-owner who conserves the public values—economic or esthetic—of which he is the custodian" (1935, 216–17).

Lean and Green

The type of private stewardship that Leopold called for was in place well before the federal government got involved. Examples abound. Indeed, Teddy Roosevelt was a founder, in 1887, of the Boone and Crockett Club, an organization that has been protecting wildlife on private lands for the past 120 years.[3] That same year the Beck family established the private Ravenna Park to preserve dwindling Douglas fir stands in Seattle (the park is home to the "Roosevelt Tree," named after the president visited the preserve).[4] In 1890 members of the Huron Mountain Club preserved thousands of wooded acres with protective covenants and hired Leopold to advise them on managing what is today one of the most pristine forests on Michigan's upper peninsula.[5] Similarly, Grandfather Mountain in North Carolina was

3. For more information on the Boone and Crockett Club, visit www.boone-crockett.org.

4. Visit www.ci.seattle.wa.us/parks/parkspaces/ravenna.htm for more information on Ravenna Park.

5. For detailed information on the Huron Mountain Club, see Anderson and Leal, 1997.

protected by Hugh Macrae, who saw a potential profit in preserving this small wilderness in the late 1800s.[6] Even Yellowstone National Park can be credited to private efforts by the Northern Pacific Railroad.[7] Motivated by a quest for passengers, the Northern Pacific lobbied Congress (Runte 1990) to set aside Yellowstone to prevent homesteading and hence an erosion of profit for the railroad if owners of Yellowstone's attractions were to charge admission.

If Leopold was correct—that individuals have the greatest responsibility and incentive to exercise stewardship over their land—then the task is to promote institutional arrangements that enable and encourage grass-roots conservancy. An example is found in 1999, when the U.S. Fish and Wildlife Service proposed creating the Aldo Leopold National Wildlife Refuge. Local Wisconsin farmers opposed the federal refuge, instead wanting to directly oversee conservation efforts and keep the land in private ownership. Working with the Fish and Wildlife Service, they formed the Farming and Conservation Together Committee—a refreshing direction for environmentalism in the twenty-first century (Norton 2003).

Despite such positive results (see additional examples in chapter 5), regulatory environmentalism is on the rise. Caught up in the competition, greener-than-thou policymakers lose sight of the fact that regulatory environmentalism has a less-than-stellar track record. The Endangered Species Act (ESA), for example, has preserved a few species but cost billions of dollars. Since 1989, the first year Congress required a report, the U.S. Fish and Wildlife Service has spent $9.7 billion enforcing the ESA.[8] The act was designed to place endangered species on a list and then, through government action, have these species delisted. Forty-one species have been removed from the list since 1973. Of those, nine were removed due to extinction, seventeen, to data error, and three were delisted thanks to the 1972 ban on the

6. For a history of Grandfather Mountain, visit www.grandfather.com.
7. See Anderson and Hill, 2004, pp. 207–8.
8. For expenditure reports, visit www.fws.gov/endangered/pubs/index.html.

overuse of DDT. What effect the ESA has had on those species who remain listed is unclear.[9]

As a result of contrived incentive structures, environmental "improvements" have sometimes created perverse results. The ESA allows the federal government to control private lands where listed species are found (more than 75 percent of endangered species depend on private land for their habitat), creating an incentive for landowners to destroy species and habitat to head off burdensome regulations. In the southeastern United States, for example, the endangered red-cockaded woodpecker has become the enemy of the landowner who cannot cut his trees if the woodpecker is found on his property. Thus timber is cut sooner than it otherwise would be to ensure that woodpeckers don't take up residence. One study found that private timber in the vicinity of abundant woodpecker colonies is harvested at seventeen years of age compared to fifty-seven years of age if there are no colonies in the vicinity (Lueck and Michael 2003). Because natural resource socialism turns woodpeckers into a liability, landowners, like any rational investor, try to minimize them (see figure 4).

In another study, University of Michigan scientists concluded that the 1998 listing of the Preble's Meadow jumping mouse prompted a backlash against the species. Their survey of affected landowners in Colorado and Wyoming discovered a disturbing trend: for every acre of private land managed to help the mouse, an acre was denuded or otherwise altered to drive the mouse away. More than half the respondents said they had not or would not let biologists survey their property, greatly hampering the collection of data needed to help the species. "So far, listing the Preble's under the ESA does not appear to have enhanced its survival prospects on private land," the researchers reported in the December 2003 issue of *Conservation Biology*. "Our results suggest that landowners' detrimental actions canceled out the efforts of landowners seeking to help the species. As more landowners

---

9. See Simmons and Frost for more details on accounting for endangered species.

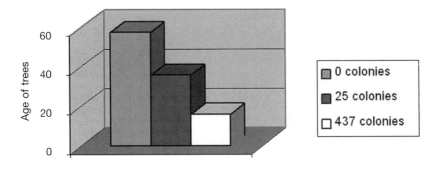

Figure 4. Harvest Age of Trees Compared to Number of Red-Cockaded Woodpecker Colonies
When the endangered bird lives nearby, landowners cut down their trees much sooner. If there are no colonies within a 25-mile radius, the predicted harvest age of trees in the area is fifty-seven years. However, if there are more than 437 woodpecker colonies in the area, the average age for harvesting trees is seventeen years.
Source: Dean Lueck, and Jeffrey A. Michael. "Preemptive Habitat Destruction under the Endangered Species Act." *Journal of Law and Economics* 46, no. 1 (2003): 27–60.

become aware that their land contains Preble's habitat, it is likely that the impact on the species may be negative."

Leopold's Legacy

Leopold was ahead of his time in realizing that incentives are more effective when they come in the form of a market carrot rather than a regulatory stick. "Conservation," he said, "will ultimately boil down to rewarding the private landowner who conserves the public interest" (1934, 202). Writing at a time when New Deal policies were at their zenith, Leopold evinced skepticism that federal conservation programs would achieve their stated aims. As he might have predicted, agricultural subsidies led to more intensive farming using more water, fertilizer, and pesticides—all with adverse environmental consequences—hardly the kind of "rewards" that Leopold had in mind.

Given their New Deal heritage, it is not surprising that Democrats have embraced regulations and subsidies as the way to direct private interests, but it is surprising that Republicans have followed this track. As Steven Hayward, a scholar at the American Enterprise Institute, points out, "the environment is for conservatives what defense is for liberals: they don't feel comfortable with it" ("Greening Bush," 2005, 34). To avoid having the environment be their Achilles' heel, Republicans have joined the greener-than-thou crusade.

But joining the green crusade is too easy. Conservationists and environmentalists of all political stripes need to find their historical roots that are anchored in substance, not form—in environmental quality, not environmental regulation. They must find ways to harness the same private incentives that drive America's economic engine to drive the environmental engine, which means rewarding rather than penalizing private stewardship. Aldo Leopold is admired by environmentalists for his "thinking like a mountain"; he should be admired by everyone for his "conservation economics."

Putting the two together allows us to move beyond greener-than-thou environmental regulation to achieve practical solutions through free market environmentalism. Leopold (1935, 255) said it well: "Conservation means harmony between man and land. When land does well for its owner; and the owner does well by his land; when both end up better by reason of partnership, we have conservation. When one or the other grows poorer, we do not."

3 You Have to Admit It's Getting Better

The race to be greener than thou is partly motivated by a concern that economic growth comes at a cost to environmental quality. As far back as the writings of the Reverend Thomas Malthus in the eighteenth century, people have worried that exponential growth in consumption would outstrip finite quantities of natural resources, ultimately causing famine, pestilence, and population decline. As noted in chapter 2, predicting that we would face a timber famine, Theodore Roosevelt put millions of acres of public domain under the control of the U.S. Forest Service in the name of sustaining our supply of wood through scientific management.

Modern environmentalists are still concerned about population growth, but now the concern is that we will foul our own nest and destroy nature in the process. The perceived conflict between economic growth and environmental quality today is embodied in the environmental buzzword *sustainability*—a word that means everything and nothing and thus offers endless opportunities to be abused. As environmental policy analyst Timothy O'Riordan (1988, 30) put it, sustainable development's "beguiling simplicity and apparently self-evident meaning have obscured its inherent ambiguity."

For many people sustainability equates to a vague notion that we should balance economic activities against natural resource use and that this balance is determined by "trained" experts. As discussed in chapter 2, this idea has been lifted verbatim from the nineteenth-century conservation philosophy of Theodore Roosevelt and his colleague Gifford Pinchot. But it seems we have already forgotten the problems of implementing Pinchot's sustained yield and multiple-use theory. As biologist David Ehrenfeld put it, "we cannot make everything best simultaneously" (quoted in Freyfogle 2006, 127). Sustainability should be viewed as a Trojan Horse that we have unwisely allowed into our homes (Freyfogle 2006, 115).

If we equate sustainability with efficient resource use and improved environmental quality, however, market economies with secure private property rights have an excellent track record. As discussed in chapter 1, Julian Simon was noted for his optimism over what human ingenuity combined with market incentives could do to ensure endless benefits from resources. In addition to the price data on the five metals included in Simon's bet with Ehrlich (see figure 5), similar trends exist with minerals throughout the twentieth century (see figures 6 and 7).

Rapid growth in demand from countries such as China and India and political instability in areas such as the Middle East can cause short-term price increases, but new supplies and substitutes mitigate against long-term increases. For example, copper wire, once used for transmitting information, has been replaced by fiber optics, satellites, and microchips. In the late nineteenth century Chile had a virtual monopoly over the production of nitrates, valued for their use in fertilizers and explosives. The high price of shipping nitrates to Europe, however, provided incentive for innovation. By the 1920s an artificial process for the production of nitrates had been invented in Germany. As a result, the price of nitrates fell so fast that even today rusty railroad cars filled with nitrates remain on the track—still waiting to be shipped to port (Minnis and Mackenzie 2004). Rising natural resource prices, coupled with secure property rights and markets, induce conservation, substitution, and technological change, all of which mitigate against the worries of doomsayers.

Furthermore, most measures of human welfare show that, on average, the world's population is better off today than any other time in human history. Life expectancy is increasing, per capita income is

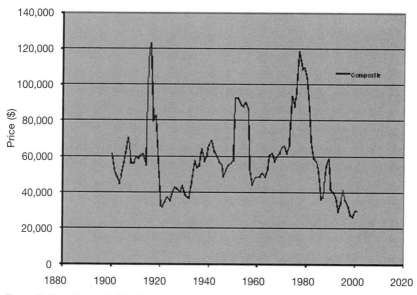

Figure 5. The Simon-Ehrlich Metals: Prices over the Century
Increased population does not necessarily cause an increase in the price of natural
resources. The composite value of the metals decreased between 1980 and 1990.
More people produced more ingenuity that overcompensated for increased demand,
and therefore prices dropped.
Source: Ross B. Emmett and David McClintick. 2005. "Betting on the Wealth of
Nature: The Simon-Ehrlich Wager." *PERC Reports* 23, no. 3: September.

rising, the air we breathe and water we drink are higher quality, and
there is more food to eat.[1] Technology and human innovation have
made life easier. These improvements have happened not just in the
United States and other developed countries but are occurring across
the entire globe.

1. The quality of water and air in the United States has greatly improved over the
last twenty-five years as we will show later in the chapter. The introduction of chlo-
rinated and filtered water to urban areas in the early twentieth century dramatically
reduced the number of waterborne diseases such as cholera and typhoid.

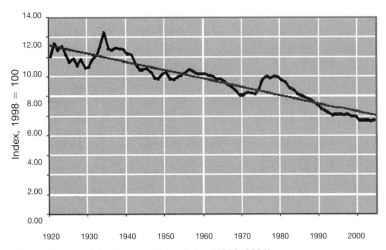

Figure 6. Industrial Minerals Price Index (1920–2004)
The Industrial Minerals Price Index is computed using data for cement, clay, crushed stone, lime, phosphate rock, salt, and sand and gravel. Together these seven minerals accounted for 88 percent of the value of all industrial minerals produced in the United States in 2004. All seven of these minerals show a declining trend in inflation-adjusted prices over the twentieth century. This declining price trend is a result of competition, reduced production costs, and adequate sources of supply (Sullivan, Sznopek, and Wagner 2000).
Sources:
Thomas D. Kelly and Grecia R. Matos. Historical Statistics for Mineral and Material Commodities in the United States. Prepared for the United States Geological Survey. Online at http://minerals.usgs.gov/ds/2005/140/ (cited July 24, 2007).
National Mining Association. Mining in the United States. Online at www.nma.org/pdf/states_04/us2004.pdf (cited July 24, 2007).
Daniel E. Sullivan, John L. Sznopek, and Lorie A. Wagner. 20th Century U.S. Mineral Prices Decline in Constant Dollars. Prepared for the United States Geological Survey and the United States Department of the Interior. Online at http://pubs.usgs.gov/of/2000/of00-389/of00-389.pdf (cited July 24, 2007).

With few exceptions, especially in areas where property rights are secure and where incomes are high and growing, environmental conditions are improving by almost any measure. In the United States, for example, air and water quality have improved dramatically during the last few decades. To be sure, we have developed new contaminants, and more-stringent regulations. For example, arsenic standards for water quality have increased, which have forced watersheds out of

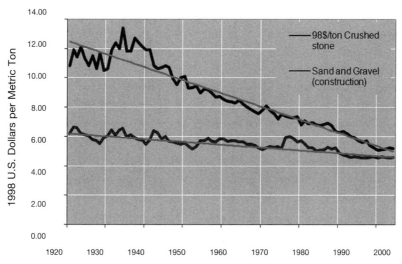

Figure 7. Price of Two Common Industrial Minerals (1920–2004)
The declining price trend of two of the most valuable industrial minerals can be seen in this figure. Crushed stone alone accounted for 29 percent of the value of all industrial minerals produced in the United States in 2004. Sand and gravel accounted for 20 percent of the value of industrial minerals produced. The declining trend in prices of these minerals suggests that they are becoming less scarce over time.
Sources:
Thomas D. Kelly, and Grecia R. Matos. Historical Statistics for Mineral and Material
     Commodities in the United States. Prepared for the United States Geological
     Survey. Online at http://minerals.usgs.gov/ds/2005/140/ (cited July 24, 2007).
National Mining Association. Mining in the United States. Online at www.nma.org/pdf/
     states_04/us2004.pdf (cited July 24, 2007).
Daniel E. Sullivan, John L. Sznopek, and Lorie A. Wagner. 20th Century U.S. Mineral
     Prices Decline in Constant Dollars. Prepared for the United States Geological
     Survey and the United States Department of the Interior. Online at http://
     pubs.usgs.gov/of/2000/of00-389/of00-389.pdf (cited July 24, 2007).

regulatory compliance, but the general trend in air and water quality has been improving in the United States. For example, between 1980 and 2006, airborne lead declined by 96 percent, carbon monoxide dropped 75 percent, and sulfur dioxide fell 66 percent (Schwartz 2008). Furthermore, open space, wildlife habitat, parklands, and so on are all in greater abundance than they were decades ago.

Despite the positive trends in environmental quality, headlines are filled with reports of environmental gloom and doom. A *Newsweek*

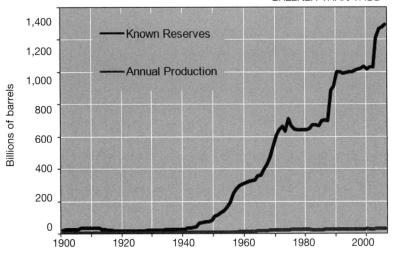

Figure 8. Known Oil Reserves and Annual Oil Production (1900–2006)
It is often claimed that the world is running out of oil. If crude oil was becoming more scarce, we would expect the amount of proven oil reserves to be falling. As the graph suggests, crude oil has become less scarce rather than more scarce. In fact, over the last century the growth of proven oil reserves has far outpaced the increase in production. Due to the expansion of oil reserves, annual production has fallen from 5 percent of reserves in 1950 to 2 percent of reserves in 2006. In 1950 you might have believed that the world would run out of oil in 20 years. So far market incentives have given us 86 more years of oil than we knew of in 1950.
Note: data from before 1944 is for the United States only.
Sources
Julian L. Simon, Guenter Weinrauch, and Stephen Moore. "The Reserves of Extracted Resources: Historical Data." *Non-Renewable Resources* 3, no.4 (May 15, 1994), 325–40. (Data for 1900 to 1978)
Marilyn Radler. *Oil and Gas Journal* 98–100, 104 (2000–2002, 2006).
Oil and Gas Journal 79–95, 101–103 (1981–1997, 2003–2005).
Auldridge, Larry. *Oil and Gas Journal* 76–78 (1978–1980): 75, 67, 99.

article entitled "Here's Dr. Doom: A Founding Father of Environmentalism Has Embraced Fatalism—and the Public Loves It" (Underhill, April 24, 2006) reviewed the latest environmental disaster tome by James Lovelock (2006). Or what about the *National Geographic*'s "By 2050 Warming to Doom Million Species, Study Says" (Roach, July 12, 2004) or *Time International*, "Look Out Below: Tourism and Global Warming Are Destabilizing Europe's Biggest Glaciers, with Potentially Disastrous Results" (Skari, July 29, 2002).

Is our natural world truly deteriorating that badly? As we shall see, the data do not support the gloom-and-doom mongering.

Malthus Meets Computers

The source of the gloom and doom can be traced to faulty reasoning and equally faulty data. Malthus argued that human population growth would ultimately run into constraints imposed by fixed natural resources, especially land for food production, which, in turn, would lead to famine and pestilence.[2] His theory fit the data of the time, namely, the population declines that occurred with the "Black Death" (1328–51).

His theory, which became known as "Malthusian cycles," captured the minds of modern environmentalists. A French riddle makes Malthus's point. Imagine a lily pond with lily pads growing so fast that the number doubles every minute. Suppose that the pond is half covered at one minute before noon. When will the pond be fully covered? Noon, of course. Now suppose you came upon the pond at 11:50 and found it only one tenth of one percent covered, will the lily pads still cover the pond by noon? Yes, with a doubling of pads every minute, the pond would be fully covered in ten minutes. And suppose you could instantly double the size of the pond, how much time would it take to cover the larger area? One minute.

By analogy, exponential population growth and rising demands for the earth's resource base will not be recognized until it is too late to act. Before a Malthusian crisis occurs, it will appear that there is no problem—the pond is less than one tenth of one percent covered at 11:50. And note that technology (the analogy to doubling the size of the pond) only buys a short amount of time.

Scientists armed with computers have refined the estimates of when crisis might set in. In 1972, a group known as the Club of Rome

---

2. For details on Thomas Malthus's ideas on human population growth, see his 1798 article "An Essay on the Principles of Population."

published a small book entitled *The Limits to Growth*. Using computer models programed with parameters similar to those of the lily pond analogy, the Club of Rome set precise dates when we would run out of resources. For example, it predicted that gold would be depleted in 1981, mercury and silver in 1985, petroleum in 1992, copper in 1993, and natural gas in 1994. The report concluded that, if the growth rates in population, industrialization, pollution, food production, and resource depletion continued, there would be "a rather sudden and uncontrollable decline in both population and industrial capacity" (Meadows et al. 1972, 56). Scary stuff.

To these predictions, Paul Ehrlich added *The Population Bomb*, a book that also said rapid population growth and consumption would lead to crises. Ehrlich wrote, "If the optimists are correct, today's level of misery will be perpetuated for perhaps two decades into the future. If the pessimists are correct, massive famines will occur soon, possibly in the 1970s, certainly by the 1980s" (1971, 24–25).

To drive the final nail into the coffin, President Jimmy Carter commissioned the *Global 2000 Report*. Again scientists, having plugged exponential population and consumption growth rates into their computers, predicted that the world would be in miserable straits by the turn of the century. The opening line of the report says, "If present trends continue, the world in 2000 will be more crowded, more polluted, less stable ecologically, and more vulnerable to disruption than the world we live in now" (Barney 1980, 1).

Whether based on lily pond riddles or sophisticated computer estimates, none of these predictions has come to pass. We have not had famine and pestilence. Rather, the percentage of the population that is starving has decreased from 35 percent to 18 percent (Lomborg 2001, 25). Wheat and corn prices have marched downward (see figure 9), and grain production is higher than ever (National Agricultural Statistics Service 2007). For the past century, innovation and technological progress have allowed the world to grow more food at a lower cost. India was perhaps, of all the developing nations, the most

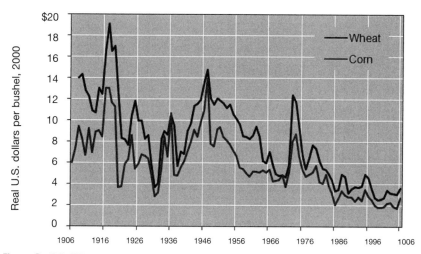

Figure 9. U.S. Wheat and Corn Prices (1906–2006)

The 1940s to the 1970s saw a revolution in food production that has allowed farmers to provide the world with more food at lower prices. The prices for grains are at all-time lows and production is higher than ever. In the United States, the real price for a bushel of corn in 2006 was $2.75, up from an all-time low of $1.77 in 2005. And the real price of a bushel of wheat in 2006 was $3.66, up from an all-time low of $2.53 in 1999. Worldwide wheat production in 2007 at 612 million metric tons, slightly down from an all-time high in 2004 of 628 million metric tons. Worldwide corn production is projected to hit an all-time high of 777 million metric tons this year (Foreign Agricultural Service 2007). The predictions of widespread famine have not come to pass.

Sources:

Foreign Agricultural Service. Grain: World Markets and Trade. Prepared by the Foreign Agricultural Service, a department of the United States Department of Agriculture. Online: at www.fas.usda.gov/grain/circular/2007/07-07/grainfull0707.pdf (cited July 18, 2007).

National Agricultural Statistics Service (NASS). Statistics by Subject: Crops and Plants. In *QuickStats* database. Washington: NASS, a department of the United States Department of Agriculture. Online at www.nass.usda.gov/QuickStats/indexbysubject.jsp?Text 1=&site=NASS_MAIN&s elect=Select+a+State&Pass_name=&Pass_group=Crops+%26+Plants&Pass_subgroup=Field+Crops (cited June 27, 2007).

successful at modernizing its agriculture production in recent times. The largest famine in modern history occurred in Bengal in the early 1940s, but, by the end of the 1970s, India had become a net exporter of wheat. The main exceptions to improved productivity are countries where tyrannical governments, not resource constraints, have destabilized economic and political institutions. Zimbabwe, for example, thanks to its despotic dictator Robert Mugabe, went from being a nation that once fed itself and exported corn and wheat to its neighbors to being one of the least productive countries in southern Africa. (Rothberg 2002).

Pound the Data

When statistician Bjørn Lomborg published his book, *The Skeptical Environmentalist*, he was attacked for finding that the environmental litany of gloom and doom does not hold up against the data. As he puts it, "When you have the data, pound the data; when you don't, pound the table." Amid the continued crescendo of table pounding, let us consider the data on various measures of natural resource use and environmental quality.

Terrestrial Resources

As noted, a combination of genetically designed high-yield crops, improved irrigation techniques, better fertilizers and pesticides, and scientific crop management has resulted in a continuous increase in agricultural productivity. According to data from the Food and Agriculture Organization (FAO) of the United Nations, world wheat production has tripled since 1961. Wheat production in 2005 was just shy of the all-time high of 2004. Wheat production in developing countries has increased from twenty-seven kilograms per capita in 1961 to fifty-three kilograms per capita in 2003—a 96 percent increase. Coarse grain production has also gone up in developing countries. In 1961, developing countries produced sixty-eight kilograms per capita; production had increased to eighty-two kilograms per capita by 2003. And increases in crop yield per acre accounted for more than 80 percent of the increase in food production in developing countries from 1961 to 2000 (Evenson and Gollin 2003, 760).

The revolution in agriculture continues to increase productivity per acre, leaving more acres for other uses, including open space and wildlife habitat. In India, for example, the *Atlantic Monthly* reported that from the 1960s through the 1980s "Green Revolution advances saved more than 100 million acres of wild lands" (Rauch 2003, 106). In fact, between 1981 and 2000 the area under cultivation in Latin America decreased 0.5 percent; overall production increased 1.6 percent (Evenson and Gollin 2003, 760). More recently, higher yields from genetically modified crops have reduced and in some cases stopped forest clearing in Honduras and the Philippines. One agricultural expert, Dennis Avery of the Hudson Institute, says that, absent improvements in farming techniques and yields since 1950, the world would have lost an additional 20 million square miles of wildlife habitat, most of it forest, to agriculture. About sixteen million square miles of forest exist today, so in a sense advances in agriculture "have saved every square mile of forest on the planet," says Avery (quoted in Rauch 2003, 106).

Indur Goklany, in his book *The Improving State of the World*, shows that, even in the face of population growth, the amount of land used for agriculture has come nowhere close to matching the growth rate in population. From 1961 to 2002, world population increased 102 percent; the land used for agriculture increased only 13 percent worldwide. One of the neo-Malthusians' greatest concerns is that population growth will require such a large amount of land to be used for agriculture that land for habitat will be lost and degraded. Such predictions of doom, once again, are not supported by the data. Advances in technology have significantly reduced the amount of land needed to feed a growing population. Goklany shows that, across the world, cropland per capita decreased by 44 percent from 1961 to 2002 and that, over the same period, food supplies per capita actually increased 24 percent (2007, 123–25).

Some of the loudest table pounding has been over deforestation. A 1998 press release from the Worldwatch Institute titled "Accelerating Demand for Land, Wood, and Paper Pushing World's Forests to the Brink" warned of a "global catastrophe." What do the data say? The FAO's *Global Forest Resource Assessment* for 2005 reports that the yearly change in forest cover has gone from −0.22 percent from 1990 to 2000 to −0.18 percent from 2000 to 2005. In many parts of the world, forest cover is increasing. The United States had more than 298 million hectares of forest cover in 1990. By 2005, that number had grown to more than 303 million hectares. Other countries, such as New Zealand, Chile, Uruguay, Spain, Russia, India, and China, have also increased their amount of forest cover during 1990–2005. The cries of a "global chainsaw massacre" (Serrill 1997) are simply not true.

Regarding endangered species, in Norman Myers's 1979 book *The Sinking Ark*, Myers estimated that 40,000 species would become extinct every year for the next twenty-five years. Myers arrived at this figure by "presuming" that one million species would become extinct over the next twenty-five years and then simply divided one million by twenty-five to get 40,000 per year. There were no data to support this presumption. Nevertheless, this number has become the official estimate of the table pounders.

Each year the World Conservation Union publishes its *Red List of Threatened Species*, the publication of record for threatened and endangered species. The 2004 edition reported that, in the past twenty years, twenty-seven species have become extinct, with another 208 possibly having gone extinct (there are no data to support that possibility). Either way, this is nowhere near the Meyers presumption of 40,000 a year. The World Conservation Union also reports that, from 2003 to 2004, 352 species were moved to a higher threat category (i.e., became more vulnerable), but 363 were moved to a lower threat category (2004). Once again the table pounding has drowned out the data pounding.

Aquatic Resources

Water covers approximately three-quarters of the earth. About 97 percent of water is found in the oceans; just over 2 percent makes up the polar ice caps, leaving less than 1 percent of earth's water available for human consumption and use. Humans currently use 18 percent of this accessible water every year (Postel, Daily, and Ehrlich 1996, 787). The World Bank's *World Development Report 1994* reported that, in 1970, 34 percent of the population of developing countries had access to safe drinking water. In the year 2000, a U.N. report by Secretary-General Kofi Annan stated that 78 percent of the population of developing countries had access to drinking water. In other words, in thirty years the percentage of the population with access to safe drinking water has more than doubled.

In addition to more people having access to water, the quality of water has improved. In the United States, the Environmental Protection Agency (2003) reported that, in 2002, 94 percent of the population got its water from systems that had no health violations, an increase from 79 percent in 1993. Also, the lakes and rivers of the United States have become cleaner. The Great Lakes, for example, which contain 20 percent of all the fresh surface water on earth, have seen a steady decline in chemical pollution since the early seventies. Between 1974 and 2005, levels of DDE, PCBs, and HCB (as measured by concentrations in herring gull eggs) declined by a minimum of 87 percent and a maximum of 99.5 percent in the various Great Lakes.[3]

3. Dichlorodiphenyldichloroethylene (DDE) is a breakdown product of DDT, which was used as an insecticide in the United States until 1972. DDE has been shown to cause liver and thyroid tumors in animals and is a probable carcinogen (Environmental Protection Agency 2007d). Polychlorinated biphenyls (PCBs) are cooling and insulating fluids. PCB production was outlawed in the United States in 1977. PCBs cause a variety of adverse health effects, including cancer and diseases of the immune system, nervous system, and reproductive system (Environmental Protection Agency

Dissolved oxygen, an essential ingredient for aquatic species and one of the best indicators of water quality, has also increased in most major rivers and lakes. For example, dissolved oxygen levels in New York Harbor have steadily improved since the 1970s (NYC Department of Environmental Protection 2003). Long Island Sound, a major area of concern for its low levels of oxygen, has seen its levels of dissolved oxygen improve. From 1985 to 2005, the area (in square miles) and duration of low oxygen levels in the sound have exhibited a downward trend (Hayward and Kaleita 2007).

The proportion of low-quality rivers in the United States and the United Kingdom, as defined by the President's Council on Environmental Quality and the Environment Agency, has also steadily declined since the 1970s (Lomborg 2001, 204). According to the Environment Agency, the percentage of bad and poor-quality rivers in the United Kingdom fell from 9.7 percent in 1990 to 4.6 percent in 2005, whereas the ratio of good-quality rivers increased by 10.3 percentage points over the same period (2007). These data suggest that access to clean water and water quality have been improving.

Atmospheric Resources

Air quality in the United States has also improved. Based on EPA data, air quality in the United States has significantly improved since 1980. Levels of nitrogen dioxide (NO_2), ozone (O_3), sulfur dioxide (SO_2), carbon monoxide (CO), and lead (Pb) all dropped between 1980 and 2006 (see figure 10). Smog was once heard about every day in the popular press and media; today, smog is only a problem in lower-income developing countries.

In addition to these improvements, particulate matter, which is made up of small solid and liquid particles suspended in the ambient air and is associated with negative health effects, has also significantly

---

2007e). Hexachlorobenzene (HCB) was used as a pesticide in the United States until 1965. HCB, a likely carcinogen, also causes liver disease and is related to several other illnesses (Environmental Protection Agency 2007f).

Figure 10. Percent Reduction in Emissions

Contaminants	1980 to 2006	1990 to 2006
NO_2	−41%	−30%
O_3 (1 hr.)	−29	−14
O_3 (8hr.)	−21	−9
SO_2	−66	−53
PM_{10} (24 hr.)	—	−30
$PM_{2.5}$ (24 hr.)	—	−17
CO	−74	−62
Pb	−95	−54

Air quality in the United States has improved significantly since 1980 as indicated by data from the EPA. The level of the common pollutants nitrogen dioxide (NO_2), ozone (O_3), sulfur dioxide (SO_2), carbon monoxide (CO), and lead (Pb) all fell over the period 1980 to 2006. Also, the level of both large and small particulate matter (PM_{10} and $PM_{2.5}$) in the air such as ash and dust, which commonly aggravate respiratory problems, fell significantly over the period 1990 to 2006.
Source: Environmental Protection Agency. Air Quality and Emissions: Progress Continues in 2006. Online at www.epa.gov/airtrends/econ-emissions.html (cited June 4, 2007).

decreased. Particulate matter comes from various sources, such as residential wood burning, coal- and oil-fired power plants, and dust particles from roads and fields. The EPA estimates that particulate matter has decreased by more than 30 percent during the past twenty-five years (2007b).[4]

The Mother of All—Global Warming

No environmental issue—terrestrial, aquatic, or atmospheric—is as powerful at mustering greener-than-thou regulations than global warming. Because greenhouse gases emitted into the atmosphere know no political boundaries and because the predicted results of global warming will affect the entire earth, the call for regulatory action is loud and clear: it is imperative that we act decisively to reduce greenhouse gas emissions. Support for this call became even stronger

---

4. More specifically, the EPA estimates that particulate matter, including particles smaller than 2.5 micrometers, has decreased by 30 percent over the past twenty-five years and that particulate matter smaller than 10 micrometers has fallen by 31 percent since 1988 (Environmental Protection Agency 2007b).

with the dire hyperbole presented in Al Gore's book and movie, *An Inconvenient Truth* (Gore 2006). Adding fuel to the fire, the third report of the United Nations' Intergovernmental Panel on Climate Change (IPCC) concludes that world temperatures are increasing and that humans are "very likely" responsible for rising temperatures (2001).

The debate over how much the earth will warm and whether the warming is caused by humans undoubtedly will continue well into the future, but whatever "the inconvenient truth," the same forces that have been improving human welfare and environmental quality throughout the world will play a crucial role in how we deal with global warming. To wit, market signals and incremental adjustments to the impacts of temperature change will dictate how catastrophic global warming will actually be. Such adjustments will come in the form of new technologies, new crops, new locations for production, and many more that are yet to be discovered.

One particularly important adjustment will come from carbon sequestration. To understand the importance of carbon sequestration, consider the difference between gross and net carbon emissions (see Anderson and McCormick 2007). Imagine two people of equal age, height, sex, and weight. Individual A consumes 3,500 calories a day, and individual B, 1,500 calories a day. On that basis, one might conclude that A is eating too much and will get fat. But suppose that A is a marathon runner and B is an office worker in a wheelchair. Without subtracting calories burned from calories consumed, we can't make predictions about whether a person will or will not gain weight. Gross intake is only half the equation.

The same is true for gross greenhouse-gas emissions. It is true that U.S. emissions have grown exponentially for at least a hundred years, but gross emissions are only half the story. The economic engine that emits greenhouse gas also sequesters it. For example, the farmer's tractor planting cotton seeds emits carbon dioxide, but the cotton seeds take up carbon as they grow. The cotton cloth produced from the seed sequesters carbon, at least temporarily and perhaps even permanently, depending on what happens to the cloth. Similarly, a growing tree consumes carbon from the atmosphere; the two-by-fours cut from that tree sequester that carbon when they are used in building homes. Instead of accusing the person who builds a second or third home of consuming too many resources, perhaps we should give him or her a sequestration award. Carbon sequestration is just as much a natural product of many commercial, industrial, and even recreational activities as carbon emissions.

Interestingly, carbon emissions per capita in the United States have been constant for the past twenty-five years (see figure 11), partly because the U.S. economy uses fossil fuels so efficiently. Hence our electricity generators, light bulbs, automobiles, and so on emit less carbon per person than in other parts of the world, and those emissions per unit of output produced have been declining.

Americans sequester nearly 40 percent of the carbon they emit (see figure 11 and McCormick, 2004). Although this has not been true for the whole of the Industrial Revolution, for the past four decades, American ingenuity and efficiency have increased the amount of carbon sequestered, thus offsetting a significant portion of U.S. emissions.

Examples of such sequestration abound. For instance, because genetically modified "Roundup ready" cotton seeds and other crops require less tilling, less carbon is disturbed in the topsoil and thus less is released into the atmosphere. Similarly, landfills, as they are managed in the United States, are enormous sequesters of carbon because the waste deposited there decays slowly; newspapers from early in the twentieth century have been dug up in virtually the same condition as when they were dumped. Those newspapers sequestered carbon that was, before the tree grew, in the air.

Although there is no guarantee that new technologies will significantly reduce gross carbon emissions or that sequestration will overtake emissions, the good news is that there is time to adjust. T. M. L. Wigley, a climatologist with the National Center for Atmospheric

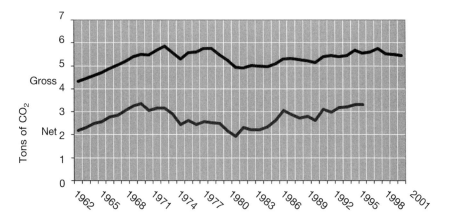

Figure 11. Gross and Net Carbon Emissions per Capita in the United States
The top line shows that carbon emissions per capita have remained relatively
constant over the past forty years in the United States. Indeed, total emissions have
been increasing, but the U.S. economy uses fossil fuels so efficiently that carbon
emissions per capita have remained constant. Still, all the carbon released does not
remain in the atmosphere. During photosynthesis, plants take in carbon dioxide and
release oxygen. Thus, plants act as natural filters of carbon, a process called carbon
sequestration. As a result of agriculture and forestry, the United States sequesters
around 40 percent of the carbon it emits. The second line of the figure reveals that
net carbon emissions are much lower than gross carbon emissions per capita.
Sources:
Terry L. Anderson and Robert McCormick. "More Inconvenient Truths." *Hoover Digest*,
   no. 2 (2007): 54–62.
G. Marland, T. A. Boden, and R. J. Andres. "Global, Regional, and National CO_2 Emissions." In *Trends: A Compendium of Data on Global Change* (Oak Ridge, TN: Carbon Dioxide Information Analysis Center, Oak Ridge National Laboratory, U.S. Department of Energy, 2002). Online at http://cdiac.esd.ornl.gov/trends/emis/
   tre_coun.htm (cited July 25, 2007).
Robert E. McCormick. "The Relation between Net Carbon Emissions and Income." In
   Terry L. Anderson, ed., *You Have to Admit It's Getting Better: From Economic
   Prosperity to Environmental Quality* (Stanford, CA: Hoover Institution Press, 2004).

Research, concludes in *Geophysical Research Letters* (1998, 2288) that the impact of reducing carbon emissions to 5 percent below 1990 levels as called for in the Kyoto Protocol "would be undetectable for many decades"; he estimates that implementing the Kyoto reductions would reduce the predicted warming from 2.5 degrees Centigrade during this century by only 0.08 to 0.28 degrees. He also states that "the prospects for stabilizing sea levels over the coming centuries are remote." Importantly, there have been no subsequent estimates to refute Wigley's conclusions.

Given that humans can do little to slow the predicted impact of carbon emissions on global temperatures and that the predicted increases in temperatures continually fall as climate models improve, the key to dealing with global warming is adaptation. Warming will occur over a long period, and humans can be remarkably adaptable if confronted with price signals from land markets, housing markets, financial markets, and insurance markets. If predictions of sea level increases are correct, the cost of living on beachfront property will increase, inducing people to move inland. Financial markets will discount rates of return for investments that do not account for the impact of global warming. And increasing weather-related insurance rates will induce people to change where and how they live.

There is already evidence of adaptation. For example, wine producers in Germany are seeing opportunities resulting from climate change. Cabernet sauvignon and merlot grapes are migrating northward, seeking cooler temperatures, which allowed German consumers to increase their consumption of locally made reds from 17 percent to 27 percent between 2002 and 2006. Complex financial instruments known as derivatives, catastrophe bonds, and sidecars allow people to hedge against volatile weather patterns ("Come Rain or Come Shine; Weather Risk," 2007). Traditionally, those instruments have been based on measures of rainfall and temperature, but they are evolving to include sea levels, wave heights, and humidity.

The challenge for greener-than-thou policymakers will be to let markets do what they do best—send price signals to consumers and producers who have secure private property rights. Politicians' responses to announcements by insurance companies that they will raise rates and cancel hurricane insurance policies in Florida and Mississippi, however, suggest that the temptation to meddle with the economy is too great. The Florida legislature, for example, considered capping insurance rates, limiting policy cancellations, and creating a $4 billion state insurance fund. Distorting such market signals is not the way to encourage adaptation. In short, we should not try to fool markets any more than we should try to fool Mother Nature.

With Every Mouth Comes Two Hands and a Brain

Just as Adam Smith's ideas might be thought of as the antidote to Malthus, the late Simon's thinking is the antidote to neo-Malthusians such as Ehrlich. Like Smith, Simon's confidence in human ingenuity came from each person's hands and brain being motivated by information and incentives. Information about increasing scarcity comes in the form of higher prices; higher prices motivate individuals to think of ways of dealing with growing scarcity; and secure property rights to scarce resources reward owners for taking action. As discussed previously, faced with the proper incentives created by property rights and markets, people conserve natural resources and improve environmental quality.

Moreover, secure property rights and markets lead to economic prosperity, which in turn provides the wherewithal for people to be environmentalists. Virtually every measure of environmental quality related to human health demonstrates a consistent relationship with income. In the early stages of economic development, environmental quality may deteriorate as citizens prefer sacrificing clean water, clean air, open space, and wildlife habitat to having food, clothing, shelter, and other consumer goods. As economic growth proceeds, environmental goods rise in citizens' priority list. With full stomachs and

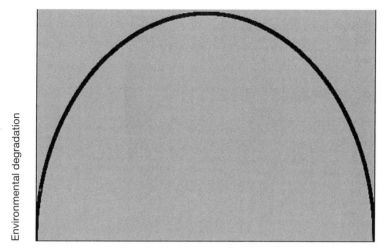

Figure 12. The Environmental Kuznets Curve
The curve shows the relationship between economic growth and environmental degradation. The curve suggests that, in the early stages of economic growth, people may be willing to degrade the environment in return for higher incomes. As income increases, however, people demand environmental quality and are willing to pay for it.

decent clothing and shelter, people begin to demand such things as clean water and air.

The relationship between economic growth and environmental quality is known as the "Environmental Kuznets Curve" (see Yandle, Vijayaraghavan, and Bhattarai 2002), named after economics Nobel laureate Simon Kuznets (see figure 12). The curve shows that in the early stages of economic growth people may be willing to give up environmental quality in return for higher incomes. But as incomes increase, people demand environmental quality and are willing to pay for it. Like it or not, we can only be environmentalists when we are wealthy enough to afford to be. Until people reach a threshold standard of living, the environmental standards to which wealthy people are accustomed are as far out of reach as fancy cars. Greener-than-thou environmental regulations that undermine prosperity undermine environmental quality, especially in the developing world. Wealthy economies such as the United States can suffer some diminished economic productivity without significantly offsetting the environmental gains, but the same cannot be said for less-vibrant economies. Hence the key to being green is promoting economic prosperity.

Ehrlich's Revenge?

When Simon and Ehrlich bet on the future of commodity prices, the data were with Simon, who was sure they would decline, but oil and food prices in 2007 and 2008 might suggest that Ehrlich would win now. Oil prices have hit all-time record highs, well over $100 per barrel, making American automobile drivers feel the sting at the gas pump. Between 1998 and 2007, the price of West Texas intermediate crude oil, a standard measure of oil prices, rose dramatically, from $55 per barrel in early 2007 to $120 in mid-2008. And rising food prices in the first half of 2008 have led to headlines announcing a "food crisis." Was Malthus right? Is the insatiable human demand outstripping Mother Nature's ability to supply?

The answer is, undoubtedly, no; Mother Nature is not the problem. Start with oil supplies. Proven reserves in the world are at an all-time high, and at current rates of consumption will last for more than a century. "We are looking at more than four and a half trillion barrels of potentially recoverable oil. That number translates into 140 years of oil at current rates of consumption, or to put it anther way, the world has only consumed about 18 percent of its conventional oil potential. That fact alone should discredit the argument that peak oil is imminent and put our minds at ease concerning future petrol supplies" (Jum'ah 2006). Of course, this longevity of oil reserves depends on rates of consumption and discovery. World per capita consumption has been steady for the last quarter century, though population growth could increase total consumption and put upward pressure on prices.

On the discovery side, it is not so much a reflection of too few dinosaurs giving their lives so that we can drive but rather a reflection of political considerations. Proven reserves continue to increase. For decades, OPEC countries, which control the vast majority of the world's oil supplies, have been limiting production to keep prices high. Coupled with this is the political instability in the Middle East which thwarts supplies and drives up prices. Iraq ranks third in proven reserves, but the Iraq war disrupted oil flows enough to influence global oil prices.

Like higher oil prices, the food crisis is partly blamed on Malthusian constraints—namely, demand outstripping supply. Again, however, such explanations are naive. On the supply side, there is nothing to suggest that agricultural productivity is declining. The level of U.S. farm output in 2004, for example, was 167 percent above the 1948 level for an average annual rate of growth of 1.74 (USDA 2008). Although higher food consumption in the developing world is being felt in the marketplace, a more likely cause of demand-side pressure is ethanol. Coupled with higher oil prices, efforts to combat carbon emissions by subsidizing ethanol production have wreaked havoc on food markets. Again, it is more politics than Mother Nature that is causing the so-called food crisis.

So if environment quality is generally improving, why is there so much environmental gloom-and-doom? At a time when more and more people are enjoying economic growth, political freedom, longer and healthier lives, more free time, and cleaner natural environments, why is there an environmental litany filled with fear? The short answer is that gloom-and-doom provides a pulpit for greener-than-thou regulatory environmentalism. This is not to say that some environmental regulations have not improved environmental quality, but it does not follow that maintaining or further improving environmental quality requires more stringent regulation.

Because there has been so much environmental improvement, new sources of environmental gloom-and-doom have risen to the surface, and global warming has become the "mother of all environmental problems." It touches us all and has become the rallying cry for "green patriotism" (Friedman 2007). As we shall see, the growing environmental bureaucracy and the special interests it serves are more often the beneficiaries of environmental regulations even when the environment is not.

4 No One Washes a Rental Car

Have you ever washed a rental car? Barring some unusual circumstance, such as the car is caked in so much mud that you can't see out the window, the answer is almost certainly, no. Unlike the rental car company, which is quick to wash, wax, and polish, we don't wash rental cars because we don't own them and thus will reap no rewards from their future rental or sale value. The owner of the car, however, by maintaining the car, captures a return in the rental and resale market.

The above analogy provides a guide for effective environmental policy. If natural resources are unowned, users have little incentive to protect them; if they are owned, long-term stewardship will follow. A report by the President's Council on Environmental Quality (1984, 363) accurately summed up this perspective: "unowned resources are more likely to be over exploited than resources privately owned and managed, since a private owner directly benefits from the preservation and maintenance of such resources and is thus more likely to act as a responsible steward." Put simply, "Tree owners are tree huggers" (Polgreen 2007).

Unowned resources, on the other hand, are subject to the "tragedy of the commons" (Hardin 1968), which originally referred to an open pasture on which any livestock owner could graze his animals. As long as there was grass to be had, animals will be grazed until the forage is gone. The tragedy is that the user has no stake in the future value and thus no incentive to preserve the resource. Hence, unowned resources are overused or undermaintained or both.

The tragedy of the commons can be seen everywhere. People litter public parks and streets more than their own yards; national forests were overlogged and now are underlogged, whereas private forests are carefully managed; landowners underprovide habitat for public wildlife yet husband land and water for domestic livestock.

Greener-than-thou policymakers rely on tragedy of the commons scenarios to justify top-down regulation, with little attention to the underlying problem of incentives and ownership. Such policies, in essence, leave the unowned car unwashed and uncared for.

The impact of ownership is shown in Brian Cromwell's study of private and public buses (1989). Cromwell found that privately owned buses were maintained better and ran longer than publicly owned buses (see figure 13). Furthermore, privately owned buses had more than twice the resale value of public buses. Similar results occur with an environmental commons, as attested by the following examples.

Home on the Range

Consider an 800,000-acre patchwork of public grazing land in Idaho's Jarbidge Resource Area, overseen by the Bureau of Land Management (BLM). Environmentalists worry about the impact that cattle grazing has on upland riparian areas and the survival of the sage-grouse (Ring 2005). Their solution is filing suit against the BLM to force it to terminate the long-standing grazing permits. That and similar lawsuits across the West have weakened the ranchers' long-term stake in the grazing areas. If they expect to lose their grazing permits, the land becomes like the unowned rental car, with no steward. And, at least in the short run, truncating grazing permits in favor of sage-grouse results in overgrazing and underproducing of grouse habitat (Watts 2006).

Contrast this scenario with media mogul Ted Turner's Flying-D Ranch, the largest contiguous private land area (110,000 acres) in the vast region around Yellowstone National Park. After Turner bought the ranch, his crews restored streambeds and are cooperating with the

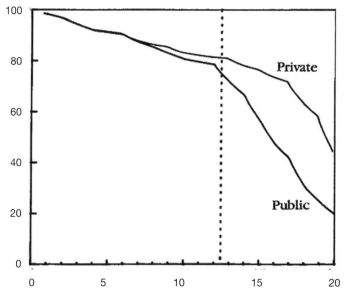

Figure 13. Private v. Public Buses
Privately owned buses last longer than publicly owned buses. Data from Brian
Cromwell show the percentage of vehicles that survive to a given age. By age 16,
less than half of public vehicles are still running whereas 73 percent of private
vehicles survive. Private owners have more incentives to protect their assets
because they capture the asset value. One would expect to see a similar pattern
for private versus public resources.
Source: Brian A. Cromwell. "Capital Subsidies and the Infrastructure Crisis:
Evidence from the Local Mass-Transit Industry." Federal Reserve Bank of Cleveland.
Q II, 1989, pp. 11–21.

state to reintroduce the threatened westslope cutthroat trout in a creek
running through his ranch. Crews removed hundreds of miles of
barbed wire fence, decrepit buildings and equipment, nonnative
weeds and grasses, and the cattle that grazed there for generations. In
the place of the cattle, thousands of bison now roam the rolling hills.
Moreover, Turner has put a permanent conservation easement on the
Flying-D that bars subdivision and limits grazing to ensure enough
forage for wildlife. Although Turner's methods have not always been
popular with the locals, there is no denying that this pristine land will
be preserved for the long term.

Turner's bison management contrasts with the management of Yellowstone National Park's bison, which are known to carry brucellosis, a virus that can cause bison and domestic cattle to abort their fetuses. Were any Montana livestock to contract brucellosis, the state could lose its brucellosis-free certification and could not ship cattle out of the state.

To ensure that his bison do not carry brucellosis, Turner vaccinates them twice a year at great personal expense. Why would he do this? First, because he reaps the value of a healthy bison herd; second, if brucellosis were transmitted to neighboring cattle, he undoubtedly would be held liable for the ensuing costs.

Although Yellowstone's bison were reintroduced to the region from fenced herds saved from extinction by entrepreneurial visionaries,[1] they are considered wild and allowed to roam freely. Some carry brucellosis. When they stray from the park, especially in the winter in search of food, they could come into contact with cattle and transmit the virus.

Unlike Turner, who vaccinates his bison and keeps them fenced in on his ranch, the National Park Service has essentially washed its hands of the problem. Once the bison cross the park boundary, the Park Service turns its responsibility over to the Montana Department of Fish, Wildlife, and Parks. That agency tries to reduce the possibility of the bison coming into contact with cattle either by scaring them back into the park or shooting them.

This illustrates what happens when ownership is not clear or when resource managers are not held accountable. Brucellosis-carrying bison are analogous to a barrel of toxic waste dumped on a neighbor's property; if the dumper is not responsible for the costs imposed on his neighbor, he has little incentive to care about the consequences. And if a rancher believes his grazing rights will be taken away, he has

---

1. For more information about how entrepreneurs saved bison from extinction, see Anderson and Hill 2004, 101.

no incentive to protect the resource. Again, no one washes a rental car.

Mixing Oil and Birds

Energy development on public lands is another environmental policy gone awry. In 1980, 1.5 million acres in the Arctic National Wildlife Refuge (ANWR) were designated as a study area in which to evaluate its potential for oil and gas development. Seven years later the Department of Interior released an evaluation recommending opening the coastal plain to gas and oil exploration. In 1995, Congress approved drilling plans, but the act was vetoed by President Clinton. At the outset of the George W. Bush administration, it was clear that the White House would pursue oil exploration and extraction from ANWR.

The national policy on drilling in ANWR has bounced around for decades, with policymakers taking extreme stands for political advantages without considering the issue in its entirety. For example, those who support drilling claim that Alaskan oil will reduce U.S. dependence on foreign sources. Senator Pete Domenici, chairman of the Committee on Energy and Natural Resources, stated that "developing oil moves us toward independence from Middle East oil. Developing this energy will stabilize energy prices and supply, easing the pressure on consumers and businesses. ANWR is and has been for some time now the right thing to do for our economy, our consumers and our energy security" (quoted in Gawell and Kagel 2006, 4). Opponents, however, quickly point out that ANWR's oil, even if it reaches its predicted peak, will satisfy less than 5 percent of U.S. demand (Utah Geological Survey 2007). And environmentalists claim that drilling in ANWR will destroy the refuge, often framing their opposition as a "righteous crusade against evil corporations out to destroy our priceless environment for short-run profit" (Lee 2005, 249). Proponents of drilling counter that the value of a pristine wilderness is often overstated. As Arctic Power (2007), an organization that promotes oil production, put it, "For most of the year, ANWR is unbearably cold and dark. For several weeks, the sun doesn't even rise and leaves the wind-swept landscape a very inhospitable environment." Clearly, extreme arguments can be made on both sides of the issue.

The real issue is ownership of the resource. Under public own-ership, there is no incentive to carefully consider the trade-offs asso-ciated with alternative or even complementary uses of ANWR. Envi-ronmental groups have no reason to take into account the benefits of drilling, and energy proponents have no drive to consider the envi-ronmental costs. Unfortunately, in the public domain, both sides stick to oversimplified exaggerations.

Consider how ownership changes the calculus. The Audubon So-ciety owns several wildlife sanctuaries, one of which is the Paul J. Rainey Preserve on the Louisiana coast. The sanctuaries fulfill Audu-bon's mission of conserving and restoring bird habitat, a goal that often generates opposition to oil exploration and development on public lands. But for nearly fifty years, Audubon allowed an oil com-pany to operate thirteen natural gas wells in the sanctuary. The oil company had to comply with tough stipulations, including no pump-ing during the nesting season and special equipment that makes less noise. In exchange, the Audubon Society earned more than $25 mil-lion and was able to buy additional land with its profits (Lee 2005).

The Audubon's Bernard Baker Sanctuary in southern Michigan is another example. When the Michigan Audubon Society purchased the sanctuary in 1941, it knew that its underground mineral rights were valuable. Oil companies initiated proposals to drill in the sanctuary in the 1960s, but this plan was protested and delayed. Eventually Au-dubon agreed to having an oil well outside its boundaries, on private property, and having the drill slant into the sanctuary's reserves, in-voking strict environmental standards to protect its birds. According to resident manager Mike Boyce (2007), the agreement earned $500,000 for Audubon; Baker is currently in negotiations with another oil company and private landowner to build an oil rig on the other side of the sanctuary. Like the rental car company that has an incentive to maintain the car while allowing it to be used, the Audubon Society has every incentive to maintain the wildlife habitat and capitalize on revenue potential.

Minding the Federal Estate

Public land is riddled with problems stemming from greener-than-thou design and management. The United States government owns a 614-million-acre estate, rich in timber, wildlife habitat, livestock forage, recreation sites, and scenic grandeur. Unfortunately, this estate is mismanaged by land agencies burdened by bureaucratic hurdles such as the regulatory morass created by laws such as NEPA (discussed in chapter 2). Although budgets for public land management have risen dramatically and land set aside for recreation and conservation has gone up, the overall quality of land has generally deteriorated. Excepting mineral production, poor fiscal management has resulted in the federal lands consistently losing millions of dollars every year (see figure 14).

Fiscal mismanagement stems from a disconnect between the amount of money spent on federal lands and the amount earned— an incentives game gone wrong. Revenue from federal lands is generally sent to the national treasury to be reallocated. In short, public land managers' spending is funded by Congress, not money generated from natural resources sales and user fees.

"Use it or lose it" policies make federal land management even more difficult. Unspent money at the end of the year does not roll over into a savings account for the following year but is instead remitted to the federal treasury. This means that managers have year-end spending sprees to ensure that they use their entire budget and therefore are less likely to face future budget cuts. Yellowstone National Park, for example, spends between 70 and 90 percent of its budget in the last two weeks of the fiscal year (Fretwell, forthcoming).

This brings us to "park-barrel" spending (Riedl 2005). Pork-

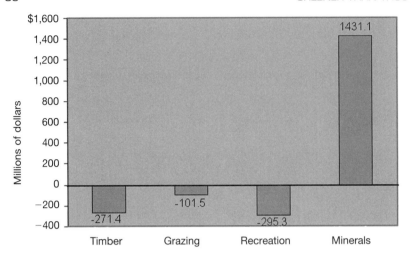

Figure 14. Average Net Returns by Activity on Federal Lands (1998–2001)
The U.S. federal lands lose millions of dollars every year on sales from timber and grazing and recreation fees. National public lands have high operating costs and low revenues. State lands, on the other hand, have much lower operating cost and make higher revenues.
Source: Holly Fretwell. *Who Is Minding the Federal Estate?* (forthcoming). Available from PERC. Data collected from the U.S. Forest Service and Burau of Land Management, 1998–2001, in 2000 dollars.

barrel projects designate tax dollars for a specific purpose to circumvent established budgetary procedures. Representatives often fund projects for which they can take credit at ribbon-cutting ceremonies and earn political points. Take, for example, the fiscal 2006 Interior Appropriations Act, which included $669.5 million dispersed among 737 new projects. One of the more egregious examples of pork was $3.3 million earmarked to construct self-composting, solar-powered toilets for a remote chalet in Glacier Park used by less than 1 percent of park visitors (Fretwell 1999). Park Service officials admitted they could put the money to better use but said they had little choice: Montana's three-member congressional delegation, reacting to a lobbying campaign by hikers, directed them to undertake the project. "We have far greater needs," said David Mihalic, Glacier's superintendent. "If somebody handed me $2.5 million and asked, 'where would you best put it?' the chalets would be far down the list. The problem is, no one did it that way. [Congress] handed us $3.3 million and said, 'put it here'" (quoted in Pound 1997). In the end, the toilets did not work so the waste is flown out by helicopter!

Pork funding, unfortunately, does not pay for unglamourous, yet crucial, maintenance programs. In March 2005, the Congressional Research Service cited $9.7 billion worth of backlogged maintenance at national parks. Cases in point: Yellowstone's outmoded sewer system allowed raw sewage to leak into native trout streams and pollute groundwater; Glacier National Park's popular Going-to-the-Sun Road is frequently closed due to safety concerns; and pre-Columbian dwellings in Mesa Verde National Park are disintegrating from a buildup of oils and airborne particles. In addition, more than one-quarter of the National Park Service's buildings are in poor or dilapidated condition (see Fretwell 2004).

Comparing federal lands to state trust lands highlights some shocking differences. In a sense, state trust managers are akin to private landowners (or rental car companies). Despite state trust lands taking on extra costs to meet strict state mandates, state agencies gain revenues for every dollar spent. Unlike federal land agencies, state trusts operate with the goal of making money and preserving their assets. In Colorado, for example, conservation leases earn the state school trust $340,000 a year. And the state of Wyoming earned more than $1.2 million from land trusts by creating conservation easements, which restrict development on state trust properties in Jackson Hole (Fretwell 2004).

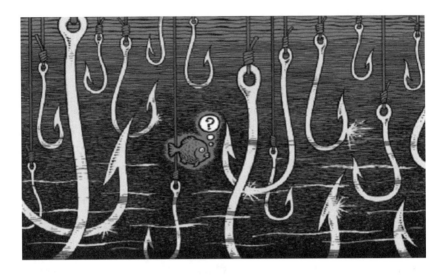

Too Many Hooks Chasing Too Few Fish

Like many ocean fisheries, that of the Alaskan halibut was threatened by overfishing in the 1980s and 1990s. In an attempt to preserve fish populations, the government put tough limits on the amount of halibut that could be caught and the length of the season. The nine-month fishing season was shortened to a few pressure-packed days during which fishers participated in a "fishing derby," pitting crews against one another and against the elements. Indeed, the movie *The Perfect Storm* demonstrates how fishing crews risk and lose their lives competing for fish in tightly regulated fisheries.

The economic impact of the derby-style fishing was devastating. Fishing crews were forced to sell their fish in a glutted market that depressed the value of their catch. Moreover, in the rush to find large halibut, crews caught whatever they could, throwing away undersized halibut and fish of other species—further decreasing future stocks.

In 1995, the Alaskan halibut fishery instituted individual fishing quotas (IFQs) to replace strict regulations and better manage the fishery. Although these quotas were not as secure as property rights, they did give each fisher the right to a portion of the total allowable catch set each season by the fishery managers, giving fishers an incentive to conserve fish stocks over the long run. Because the quotas are transferable, quota holders can buy and sell quotas from other fishers, thus maximizing the size of their boats and companies.[2]

In the first year under IFQs, the fishing season expanded from two days to eight months. Bycatch (species other than those under quota) was reduced more than 80 percent, fishing crews earned higher prices for their catch, and, with annual shares safe in the water, crews stayed home during bad weather so that not a single life was lost (O'Keefe 2004). Thus fishing quotas changed anglers' perspective from treating the fishery as a commons to be exploited to husbanding it as a valuable asset to be sustained. The Alaskan experience is just a small sample of what ownership can do; worldwide, at least 100 marine species are now under individual fishing quota management (Leal 2006).

Superfund a Superwaste

Superfund, the common name of the Comprehensive Environmental Response, Compensation, and Liability Act (CERCLA), was passed in 1980 to clean up hazardous waste sites that endangered public health. Under CERCLA the EPA was given a $1.6 billion trust fund with which to clean up sites and charge responsible parties. Both previous and current owners of the sites are required by law to compensate the government for the cleanup costs once notified of the EPA's charges.

The courts try to ensure that the EPA's actions are not arbitrary or capricious and that the agency accepts public comment, but the courts are also unable to limit the fines set by the EPA, allowing the EPA to garner unlimited sums of money. Case in point, in a quarry west of Tulsa, Oklahoma, the EPA charged $12 million to clean up the abandoned Compass Industries Landfill Site. The local State De-

2. A more detailed explanation of individual fishing quotas (IFQs) is available at www.ifqsforfisheries.org.

*"Miss Endicott, I spilled ketchup on my tie.
Have the government clean it up."*

partment of Health concluded that $1 million would have been sufficient to contain the waste and provide a cost-effective, permanent cleanup (Office of Technology Assessment 1988).

Allowing the EPA such discretion removes the incentive for a rational calculation of costs and benefits.[3] The EPA has declared 55,000 waste sites as potential hazards but is not required to provide evidence of the harm done or direct links to the parties held responsible (Stratman 2000). Former EPA director of waste programs enforcement, Bruce Diamond, claimed that "an aging truck driver who says, 'I took yellow liquid and I think it was from them'" (quoted in Bovard 1994) is all the evidence necessary to declare a site eligible for Superfund.

3. Online at www.yale.edu/esi/ESI2005_Main_Report.pdf.

In Minneapolis, for example, the EPA held a local Boy Scout troop financially responsible for cleaning up a Superfund site because the troop had disposed of metal at the local scrap yard (Bovard 1999). Moreover, there is evidence that the amount spent on cleanup bears a stronger relationship to campaign contributions for senators and members of Congress than it does to how hazardous the site actually is (see Stratmann 2000).

In contrast, private companies who have begun cleaning up waste are making a profit doing so. The Remediators, for example, a company in Port Angeles, Washington, uses a biological process to clean private residential and commercial properties thought to be contaminated. The company, which focuses primarily on petroleum contamination, relies on fungi's ability to naturally decompose organic compounds and return the soil to a healthy state. With approximately 21,000 known abandoned contaminated sites rendering more than 81,000 acres of land practically useless, the Remediators can identify those sites, restore their economic value, and resell them at a profit. The company, landowners, and community all benefit from using privately administered fungi as an alternative to expensive and long-term mechanical or chemical treatments.[4]

Beware of the Greenwagon

Before you board the trendy greenwagon, be aware of the unintended consequences that can be bad for the economy and the environment. Greener-than-thou policymakers love to tout environmental solutions, but measuring their actual impact and outcome is often problematic.

The inherent complexity of environmental problems makes it difficult to foresee how regulations will play out. When fishing seasons were shortened to reduce overfishing, fishers took more risks by fishing in foul weather, using larger boats, and employing sophisticated

4. For more information about the Remediators, visit www.theremediators .com/, and see the December 2006 Enviropreneur issue of *PERC Reports.*

electronic gear to catch more fish in the shortened season. When fuel efficiency standards are imposed on new cars, making them more expensive, people drive their old cars, which pollute more. When zoning restrictions raise housing costs, developments move out of the zoning district. When the ESA regulates those whose land harbors endangered species, the landowners eliminate the habitat before the species are discovered or can move in. No matter how many fingers regulators put in the holes of the regulatory dikes, those who are regulated are apt to react in unanticipated ways.

The tendency of politicians to favor special interests is also problematic for the environment and for the public interest, of which the Clean Air Act amendments of 1977 are a blatant example. Those amendments required that new coal-fired power plants install scrubbers costing millions of dollars in hopes of reducing acid rain. Not surprisingly, the amendments were supported by environmental groups. Existing power plants were "grandfathered," meaning they did not have to install the scrubbers. Hence, established plants supported the amendments because the new costs were imposed on new, competing plants. The unintended consequence was that plants reduced their use of cleaner, low-sulphur western coal, making electricity more expensive and the air dirtier because the old plants burned dirty eastern coal (Ackerman 1981). To this day, if older plants want to become more efficient, they must install expensive scrubbers; therefore they continue to operate antiquated equipment. When the Bush administration tried to relax these requirements to promote more efficient and cleaner technology, it was vilified by many environmentalists (Schwartz 2003). That well-intentioned environmental policies often fall short of their goals is a compelling reason to seek new approaches to environmental problems.

To be sure, some greener-than-thou regulations can and have improved environmental quality. The Clean Water Act and the Clean Air Act targeted egregious cases of water and air pollution. The Wilderness Act established wilderness areas off-limits to all mechanized activities. And the ESA stopped the blatant killing of species such as the bald eagle. But picking off those low-hanging environmental fruit was easy. To reach the higher fruit on the environmental quality tree, we will have to be more innovative. Such innovation will only emerge if we can make stewardship and environmental quality an asset rather than a liability, the focus of chapter 5.

5 Markets Are a Frog's Best Friend

Kermit the Frog would have found it easier to be green had he discovered markets and private stewardship, as did his relative, the endangered Houston toad whose friend, rancher Bob Long, describes himself as a "gun toting, redneck, Texas Republican preacher" (McMillan 2003, 5). To that list he should add free market environmentalist. Through the Leopold Stewardship Fund and a Safe Harbor Agreement under the Endangered Species Act, Long has helped provide habitat for the toad. The Leopold Stewardship Fund paid for the fences Long built to keep his cattle away from the toad-breeding ponds and native plants. The Safe Harbor Agreement afforded him protection from onerous land-use regulations that make endangered species the enemy (Environmental Defense 2003). Under the Safe Harbor Agreement, Long agreed to manage his ranch so as to promote Houston toad habitat in return for a guarantee from the U.S. Fish and Wildlife Service that additional endangered species regulations will not be imposed on him. (See chapter 6 for details on safe harbor agreements.)

Market-enabling tools such as the Leopold Fund and the Safe Harbor Agreement are making the environment an asset rather than a liability. As a sage Montana rancher put it, "If it pays, it stays." Positive incentives provide carrots that often are more effective than regulatory sticks for encouraging environmental quality. Sometimes regulatory sticks may be necessary, but they usually ignore the incentive potential inherent in market carrots.

Going Global

Before considering more examples of how markets can work in the United States, we must point out that free market environmentalism is a worldwide phenomenon. Making the environment an asset is essential, especially in the developing world, where people living in nature have not yet reached the level of wealth necessary to afford them the time to think about being green.

Land of Milk and Honey

Market solutions have been proven effective even in countries where property rights are poorly defined and often not enforced. In the Los Negros Valley in Bolivia, downstream farmers didn't have enough water for their crops, largely owing to upstream deforestation in the cloud forest of Amboro National Park—a unique ecosystem that creates moisture. As the forest cover was reduced, the Los Negros River began drying up earlier and earlier each year. Although it is illegal to cut down trees in a buffer zone along the river, upstream dwellers often cut timber wherever they please. Given Bolivia's poor legal institutions and insecure property rights, downstream landowners had to find another solution to enhance their decreasing flows.

Natura Bolivia, an environmental group, helped resolve the conflict using a system of payments for environmental services (PES). Through negotiations, Natura Bolivia agreed to compensate the upstream landowners to preserve native vegetation, with payment in beehives and training in honey production. The upstream loggers receive one hive for every ten hectares of water-producing forest they protect. Since PESs were introduced, upstream participants have begun requesting some of their compensation in the form of barbed wire with which to confine their livestock and to clearly define property boundaries and land claims.

The upstream landowners and downstream water users' agreement has not been without its problems. Lacking a well-entrenched rule of law, creative solutions had to be found to enforce the contracts for watershed services. To clearly define property rights, Natura Bolivia used Global Positioning Systems and natural boundaries, such as rivers and mountains, to draw property boundaries. To enforce the contract, Natura Bolivia has declared that it will not renew the contract if either party fails to comply with the terms. To determine how much additional water has resulted from upstream forest preservation, landowners measure water depth, stream flow, velocity, and rainfall.

The above demonstrates how market solutions can mitigate conflict over environmental resources and have the potential for producing ecosystem services. Even in Bolivia, which lacks an effective legal system and property rights, market solutions have generated gains from trade for both loggers and farmers.

Tree Owners Are Tree Huggers

How can Niger, an African country with an exploding population growth and ongoing hunger, have added 7.4 million acres of tree-covered ground since 1980? The answer is that landowners now own the trees on their land. In the past, all trees were owned by the state, meaning that the landowners had little incentive to preserve them. Just as no one washes a rental car, no one took care of the trees in Niger. Little thought was given to the environmental costs of harvesting trees for firewood or for construction. Farmers cleared vegetation from their fields, including trees, before planting rows of crops. When the land became less productive, the farmers moved to new plots, leaving behind land devoid of trees. Although government forest regulators were supposed to conserve the trees, they were ineffective in stopping the farmers from clearing trees for their crops.

In 1974, the Niger government, turning to a property rights approach, allowed individuals to own the trees on their land. As a result of both the change in the law and a severe drought in the late 1970s and early 1980s that wiped out vast stands of trees, farmers realized how scarce trees had become and began conserving them. Farmers and other landowners began cultivating six species of trees that would provide them with additional income. Now landowners can sell branches, pods, fruit, bark, and leaves. Not only have the revenues increased farmers' incomes, but they have softened the ups and downs of farming in such a drought-prone environment.

Tree ownership has also positively affected the lives of women and youth. Women who used to spend more than two and a half hours a day gathering firewood now spend just half an hour. More youth stay in their home villages rather than leave for the city because they can earn money by taking forest products to market (Larwanou, Abdoulaye, and Reij 2006). Thus, assigning property rights to private landowners has given them the incentive to improve the environment; their trees are now an asset.

The Northern Jaguar

Jaguars once roamed much of the southwestern United States but were killed off in the past century as ranchers began raising cattle in the region and as federal programs were introduced to eliminate predators that preyed on livestock and other wildlife. The last known jaguar in the United States was shot near the Grand Canyon in 1963. A population of jaguars has survived in northern Mexico, but these too have become increasingly persecuted by ranchers and poachers. In the past two years, ranchers have killed more than twenty jaguars, including females and kittens. Some environmental groups have lobbied the U.S. government to create protected habitat for the jaguars in New Mexico and Arizona along the Mexican border, but these efforts have met resistance from ranchers in the region and thus been unsuccessful to date.

One group, however, is using the market to create a jaguar reserve. The Northern Jaguar Project, in conjunction with Naturalia and Defenders of Wildlife, purchased a 10,000-acre ranch in Sonora, Mexico, where cattle ranching is the principal activity in the rough, rocky mountains. To expand its reserve, partners are currently trying to buy an adjacent 35,000-acre ranch. The money to carry out this project is donated by private individuals and organizations interested in preserving the northern jaguar (Nistler 2007).

Because a male jaguar's territory can encompass more than 500 square miles, the Northern Jaguar Project is also working to protect jaguars who venture outside the reserve. The project considered a compensation program for cattle killed by jaguars, modeled after the one used in wolf reintroduction (see below), but the area is so remote that it is almost impossible to determine what has killed the cattle, much less find the dead animal.

Instead, the Northern Jaguar Project has launched the "Save a Spot" program that has paid for automatic cameras to be installed on nearby ranches, paid local vaqueros to maintain the cameras, and paid compensation for ranchers. When a jaguar is photographed on private land, the ranch owner receives as much as $500—making the jaguar worth more alive than dead (Friederici 2006).

Rather than governments' forcing landowners to comply with conservation regulations, market solutions such as those used by the Northern Jaguar Project serve the interests of both landowners and conservationists. The ranchers of the Sonora have an economic rationale for protecting the jaguar, and, as a result, they have become wildlife-friendly vaqueros. Through these efforts, it is possible that people in North America may start seeing the spots of the jaguar again.

Into Africa

The Communal Areas Management Program for Indigenous Resources (CAMPFIRE) program effectively preserves wildlife in southern Africa, primarily in Zimbabwe, despite Robert Mugabe's corrupt regime. Previous conservation efforts on communal lands had been inadequate. Communal lands, generally the least productive land for agriculture, often border areas designated for wildlife, creating a potential conflict between farmers and such wildlife as elephants, buffalo, crocodiles, rhinos, and leopards that eat crops, livestock, or humans. Occupants of communal lands therefore view these animals as the enemy and seek to eliminate them. As a result, poaching has decimated wildlife populations as farmers try to protect the land and livestock they need to earn even subsistence incomes.

Programs such as CAMPFIRE recognize that people will preserve wildlife if they benefit from its presence. To accomplish this goal, the national government has transferred wildlife management to representatives of the small villages. Although the property rights are not directly held by the village, a district council representing the village controls the wildlife and the income generated from preserving it. Through this devolution of property rights, the people living with the wildlife gain from conserving it.

Under the CAMPFIRE program, wildlife populations and wildlife habitat have increased significantly. Elephant populations in Zimbabwe, for example, have grown from 89,000 to 119,000 since 1979 (Kanhema 2006), even though trophy hunting of elephants has almost doubled (Hess 1997). Countries with local communities that profit from wildlife viewing and hunting, such as South Africa, Zimbabwe, and Botswana, contain the continent's only increasing elephant populations (Kanhema 2006). To promote habitat, villagers are cutting fewer trees, grazing fewer cattle, and lighting fewer bush fires.

One problem with CAMPFIRE-type programs is that some of Africa's potential wildlife habitat has been set aside in national parks (see Hess 1997), meaning that too often local people, living at or near the subsistence level, are evicted from their traditional land and forced to compete with wildlife that migrates from the parks and consumes neighboring grazing and cropland. Moreover, the primary beneficiaries of national parks are wealthy foreign tourists and the concessionaires who supply transportation, lodging, and food for the ecotourists.

Recognizing the problem, groups such as the African Wildlife Foundation (AWF) and the Nature Conservancy are experimenting with leasing land from local groups for wildlife habitat. Near Nairobi National Park, for example, AWF is paying families $4 per acre per year to not cultivate the land, instead only grazing it and protecting wildlife on it (see Dunkel 2007). From two families and 214 acres in 2000, the program has grown to more than 100 families and 8,500 acres in 2007. Patrick Bergin, CEO of AWF, notes that "private land conservation has had an amazing impact in North America. My feeling is that this conservation approach has great potential in Africa—the surface has not even been scratched" (quoted in Dunkel 2007, 25). Although Bergin is correct in saying that private land conservation in North America has done a lot, the surface in the United States has not been scratched either.

YIMBY (Yes, in My Backyard)

Markets are being applied in many parts of the developing world because people there cannot afford to be environmentalists unless it pays. As mentioned earlier, high incomes are a driving force of demands for environmental quality. People living at or near subsistence levels cannot afford to preserve land for environmental amenities or clean up their air and water at the expense of economic development. Not surprisingly, in the developing world laws mandating greener-than-thou regulations are simply ignored.

Policymakers in rich countries such as the United States, however, can afford to pass and enforce environmental regulations, regardless of their costs or effectiveness. High incomes make it easy to be greener than thou without worrying about how efficacious the regulations are. As we saw in chapter 4, Superfund legislation spent billions of dollars cleaning up toxic waste sites with a relatively small bang for the buck; the Endangered Species Act has cost billions, not counting the costs imposed on landowners and the unrecovered species; and efforts to remove minuscule amounts of arsenic from the nation's water will cost billions, all in the name of reducing cancer risks by imperceptible amounts.

Popular bumper sticker in Montana

Moreover, in many cases, despite the billions of dollars spent, adversaries battle over the right way to produce environmental quality while the environment suffers. Timber management on federal lands is tied in such a "Gordian knot," to use the words of President Clinton's chief of the Forest Service, Jack Ward Thomas, that wildfires rage while environmentalists sit in air-conditioned courtrooms. "No moo in '92" and "cattle free in '93" were slogans aimed at removing cattle grazing from public lands during the Clinton administration, but grazing policies changed little.

Pragmatic environmentalists who realize that rhetoric and regulations are often ineffectual are now "finding the ways that work," to use the motto of Environmental Defense Fund. When pragmatism supplants green rhetoric, environmental quality flourishes, as the following examples attest.

Cows not Condos

"Cows not Condos," the motto of the Montana Land Reliance (MLR), a land trust devoted to using privately negotiated conservation easements to preserve farmland and agricultural values, says a great deal about the trade-offs pragmatic conservationists must face.

MLR works with hundreds of farmers and ranchers to place nearly half-a-million acres under easements restricting uses to agriculture and silviculture, yet allowing the landowners to manage their lands. The government gives the landowner tax deductions equivalent to the difference between the unrestricted and restricted values of the land;

otherwise the easements are voluntary transactions that preserve Montana's farm and ranch culture and provide open space and wildlife habitat.

The MZ–Ranch, located near Belgrade, Montana, exemplifies what private landowners can do for conservation even without tax deductions. The MZ allows us to have our fish and graze it, too. On the ranch owned by Tom and Mary Kay Milesnick, the third generation on the property, dozens of Angus cows and calves graze the banks of Thompson and Ben Hart Spring Creeks and others stand in the water for a drink. Across the fence, neighboring acres are growing condos, not cows.

Many anglers think cows and fishing cannot mix, but the Milesnicks are proving them wrong. In the past, the crystal clear waters of Thompson and Ben Hart Spring Creeks were primarily used to water cows, with fish taking a backseat. With cattle wading, drinking, and excreting everywhere, fishers only had a few pools into which they could cast a fly. Like many Montana ranchers, Tom and Mary Kay were willing to share the stream with fishers, but their cattle came first.

As the Milesnicks cattle were having the run of the stream, other spring creek owners were capitalizing on the fishing boom sparked by the movie *A River Runs through It*. In the Paradise Valley, south of Livingston, Montana, for example, three spring creeks were charging fishers upward of $100 per day. Because the streams had become such valuable assets, the cattle took a backseat, with fences keeping the bovines away from riparian areas.

But fencing is expensive, and Tom hoped to find a way whereby his cows and the fish could share the water. His experience as a rancher told him that cows do not like standing in mud, which results when the streambanks sluff into the water and fill it with silt. To eliminate the mud and entice the cattle to drink in selected areas, Tom laid gravel pads on which the cattle could wade into the creek without destroying the banks and causing siltation. He also discovered that intensive grazing at certain times of the year keeps the weeds along the banks down and allows native grasses to thrive and hold the banks in place.

Now Mary Kay charges fees ($75 per fisher per day) and limits the number of fishers each day. Because the fishing is so good, the MZ–Ranch is booked a year in advance. More important, the revenues the Milesnicks collect from fishing augment traditional ranching revenues to keep the land in "cows not condos." When asked what share of the revenues comes from fishing, Tom says only 8 percent, at which point Mary Kay smiles and notes that those revenues account for 40 percent of the ranch's net income because, after the initial investment, there are few costs (Grewell 2002).

Some might say that the Milesnicks should not profit from nature because nature belongs to us all, but profitability leads to sustainability. As more ranchers capitalize on their amenities, they will become the green thumb in Adam Smith's invisible hand. As Smith put it, when an individual pursues his or her own interests, "he is in this led by an invisible hand to promote an end which was no part of his intention. By pursuing his own interest he frequently promotes that of the society more effectually than he really intends to promote it."

A Sheep in Wolf's Clothing

Market solutions are also working to resolve conflicts between conservationists wishing to protect grizzly bears and wolves and ranchers trying to make a living from cattle and sheep. Hank Fischer, who created the Proactive Carnivore Conservation Fund while working for Defenders of Wildlife, has expanded the use of market tools to protect wolves and grizzly bears in the greater Yellowstone area, which can pose serious problems for ranchers who graze sheep near wolf and grizzly habitat.

The Proactive Carnivore Conservation Fund provides money to help prevent wolf and grizzly predation from occurring by working with ranchers to create prevention mechanisms such as a secure night pasture for sheep, bear-proof garbage receptacles, and alternative sheep- and cattle-grazing areas where there are no wolves or grizzlies. In 2006 Fisher helped retire 74,000 acres from a grazing allotment in the Gallatin National Forest on which, between 1999 and 2003, bears and wolves had killed more than a hundred sheep. Representing the National Wildlife Federation, Hank paid the rancher $130,000 to move his sheep from harm's way. As Hank put it, "We aren't getting rid of grazing; we're redistributing where it occurs—away from core wildlife areas near national parks and wilderness areas and closer to low-conflict areas" (Stark 2006). In three years, Fischer's program has retired more than 300,000 acres of grazing allotments near Yellowstone National Park.

Fish in the Sea

Gordon Fox had been making his living as a bottom-trawling fisher (dragging a net along the ocean floor to catch fish) off the coast of California for years. Owing to bottom trawling's negative effects, however, six species of ground-fish had become severely depleted. Environmentalists initially tried to block fishing with a lawsuit, which failed and, like all lawsuits, created tremendous animosity. The judge in the case ordered the National Marine Fisheries Service to prepare an environmental impact statement, which opened the door for some healing market ointment. Environmentalist Chuck Cook (who has been called a "conservation Nazi"), Rod Fujita, a marine scientist with Environmental Defense Fund, and fishers began working together to develop and submit a plan to preserve the fish (see Christensen 2006).

The accepted plan provided a win-win alternative, with the Nature Conservancy and Environmental Defense Fund teaming up to buy fishing permits and boats from local fishers and, in exchange, fishers agreeing not to bottom trawl in vulnerable areas. Five of the six trawling permits in Morro Bay were purchased by environmental groups, generating several hundred thousand dollars each for the permit holders. The environmentalists are also trying to purchase an additional ten permits from northern bays. Using markets, environmentalists and fishers have preserved 3.8 million acres of ocean off the coast of central California—an area roughly the size of Connecticut.

In the future, the Nature Conservancy and Environmental Defense Fund plan to lease permits back to fishers with stipulations designed to protect the fish populations and biodiversity in the area. Those leases will be similar to land conservation easements, which have stipulations as to how the land will be developed. In the fishing case, restrictions will be put in place on the type of equipment that can be used for fishing, the areas that can be fished, and the species that can be harvested.

Through solutions such as these, an estimated two-thirds of the overall biodiversity along the coast of central California has been preserved. Like individual fishing quotas (IFQs) (see chapter 4), markets are proving much more effective than regulations in promoting sustainable fish stocks and biodiversity.

Trust Us for Water Conservation

Mark Twain supposedly said, "Whiskey is for drinkin' and water is for fightin'," and if he didn't he surely would if he were writing about water use today. As municipal and environmental demands for water have grown, conflicts over water have increased. Especially in drought years, claims to divert water exceed stream flows. Famous cases such as the dispute between Los Angeles and the Mono Lake Committee over the diversion of water from streams feeding Mono Lake in the eastern Sierras to a tube 225 miles south to Los Angeles are not unique. In this case bumper stickers from the early 1980s, which declare that the country's oldest and most unusual lake is being destroyed, can still be seen. Thousands of competing claims for water have reduced instream flows and increased the flow of litigation (Libecap 2007).

One reason for conflict is that the prior appropriation doctrine, which governs water use in the West, typically requires that water be diverted from the stream lest the water right be forfeited and claimed by another diverter; in other words, "use it or lose it." Under that doctrine those holding a water right could not opt to leave the water in the stream to ensure stream flows because instream flows are not considered a "beneficial use" of water, thus encouraging the overuse of water and discouraging the development of water markets (see Anderson and Snyder 1997).

As Bob Dylan put, however, "times they are a changing." Just as miners and farmers hammered out the prior appropriation doctrine in the late nineteenth century, market-minded conservationists are refining that doctrine to allow them to engage in willing buyer–willing seller water trades to increase instream flows. States such as California, Montana, and Oregon have changed their water laws to allow water to be leased to improve aquatic habitat. Other states such as Colorado, Idaho, and New Mexico have authorized their state agencies to appropriate, buy, or lease water for instream flows where it is critical for a healthy aquatic ecosystem (Scarborough and Lund 2007).

The result of this forward thinking has been less money spent on lobbying and lawsuits and more spent on getting water in the stream. For example, in the case of Mono Lake, it took fifteen years of litigation before water began to flow back into the lake, even then the flows have been far short of environmental goals. Water levels in Mono Lake have increased by nine feet, but this is a far cry from the twenty feet required by the state's ruling. Had the Mono Lake Committee entered into market transactions to increase the lake's level, restoration would most likely be much farther along (Libecap 2005 and 2007).

By harnessing water markets to save our streams, we can have "whiskey for drinkin' and water for fishin'." In ten western states approximately $300 million has been spent on more than a thousand water transactions to restore stream flows between 1998 and 2005. The result is six million more acre-feet of water devoted to instream flows, enough to cover the state of New Hampshire with one foot of water (Scarborough and Lund 2007).

"For the Benefit and Enjoyment of the People"

Those words are carved on the Roosevelt Arch, the gateway to the north entrance of Yellowstone National Park. Although, as we noted in chapter 2, the park was not created by Teddy Roosevelt, he did visit the park in 1903 to dedicate the arch, saying, "Yellowstone Park is something absolutely unique in the world. . . . This Park was created and is now administered for the benefit and enjoyment of the people. . . . [I]t is the property of Uncle Sam and therefore of us all."

Unfortunately, the park and many other recreational assets that are "the property of Uncle Sam" have been treated too much like rental cars; they are overused and undercared for. Although national forest deficits are larger for recreation than for any of the other major land uses, users complain that more needs to be spent on recreation (see chapter 4). For example, in 2005, after the Bush administration revised downward the estimates of how much recreation in national forests contributes to GDP, Frank Hugelmeyer, president of the Outdoor Industry Association, contended that those estimates were too low. Arguing that national forests' contribution to GDP is 2.5 to 4.0 times more than commodity production from the same forests, he concluded that "staffing and funding for recreation in the agency [U.S. Forest Service] doesn't match up to this reality" and that spending on recreation management and trials is "woefully inadequate" (2005).

Similarly, national park supporters call for larger budgets to cover both operating and capital expenditures. In February 2007, the National Parks Conservation Association launched a campaign called Make National Parks a National Priority. Some 40,000 activists signed petitions asking Congress to increase national parks funding. To their delight, the 2008 House Interior Appropriations bill budgeted $2.5 billion for the NPS, a $223 million increase from 2007. The National Parks Conservation Association website said, "This is *great* news for

Congestion in Zion National Park

our national parks, providing much-needed funding to maintain hiking trails, restore critically-needed visitor services, including guided tours and educational programs, address park-related expenses and fill more than 3,000 seasonal ranger positions which had been lost over the years to budget crunches" (House Budget 2007).

Despite these calls from special interest groups for more spending, indications are that recreation on public lands is subject to the tragedy of the commons. Try to find a place to photograph Old Faithful without getting another person's head in the picture; try to find a campground or a room in Yosemite in the summer without reservations far in advance; try to find a trailhead to a popular wilderness area that is not packed with cars; or try to find a place to hunt on public lands on the opening day of the hunting season that is not overrun with other hunters. Indeed, recreation on public lands is down in many cases, and part of the reason for the decline is dissatisfaction with the recreational experience. *Consumer Reports* found that overcrowding and facility maintenance are the top concerns of park visitors (1997).

Yosemite National Park closes the park entrance several times a year because of gridlock in the valley. On average, 6,500 cars arrive at the South Rim of the Grand Canyon, but there are only 2,400 parking spaces (see Fretwell 1999). And Zion National Park implemented a mandatory shuttle bus system to reduce traffic congestion.

As crowding and overuse have grown on public lands, entrepreneurs have turned their attention to recreational profit opportunities. When Roosevelt visited Yellowstone in 1903, guest ranches provided city slickers with a chance to experience the Old West. As mentioned in chapter 2, in the late nineteenth century, long before environmentalism was fashionable, private entrepreneurs in Seattle were saving giant old-growth Douglas fir trees from sawyers. In Oregon, Sea Lion Caves were protected by an entrepreneur who capitalized on nature by protecting the sea lion habitat and providing viewing opportunities to tourists.

Today the entrepreneurial spirit lives on, despite that fact that it must compete against low-cost or even free recreational opportunities provided by local, state, and federal governments. Consider this short list of examples.

Rock climbing—When most people think of rock climbing, they think of Yosemite National Park where El Capitan, Half Dome, and Lost Arrow tower above the valley floor. To climb these faces, however, requires more than skill; it requires queuing to get your place to start a route and then racing to stay ahead of following climbers. Human feces are not uncommon on ledges, chalk used to keep hands dry marks routes, and sometimes equipment is left on the routes.

Although climbers may aspire to Yosemite, most climb smaller faces closer to home, many of which are found on private land. An excellent example is Laurel Knob, a 1,200-foot towering rock on forty-seven acres of private property surrounded by upscale home sites in North Carolina. The owner, Dr. Tom German of Charleston, South Carolina, was not fond of having climbers trespass on his property

Traffic jam on the cables on Half Dome in Yosemite National Park

because climbers often placed permanent anchors and bolts on the rock and because liability for the private landowner can be scary.

The Carolina Climbing Coalition (CCC) came to the rescue. Led by John Myers, an avid rock climber and experienced conservationist, in 2006 the CCC negotiated with German to purchase the Laurel Knob property for $5,000 per acre, substantially less than the going price (in the area of $15,000 per acre). In seven months the CCC raised $100,000 from people in thirty-five states and seven foreign countries. As a nonprofit organization, the CCC is hosting fund-raisers to pay off the $150,000 loan. A member of the coalition, Harrison Shull, notes that "this [purchase] legitimizes groups like mountain bikers, paddlers and climbers. Not only do we know what we're doing, but it proves we can make things happen" (quoted in Chavez 2006).

Mountain biking—Proving Shull's point, some entrepreneurs are building mountain bike parks. Andy Myers, for example, recently converted a private landfill near the airport in Tempe, Arizona, to a slalom biking course. The route offers bikers a thrill, dropping 50 feet in 22 seconds. And rancher Paul Nolan's friends convinced him to turn some of his horse trails into mountain biking trails. Now he rents out his ranch to the Houston Area Mountain Bike Riding Association for bike races. Fellow Texas rancher Trey Hill now supports himself full time with a bike resort that offers forty miles of trails, camping facilities, trailer hookups, and a restaurant. He also holds a renaissance festival each year and is working on hosting outdoor concerts. Typically, around 150 riders come every Saturday.

Golf—Hazards on fairways take on a new meaning when you realize that entrepreneurs are taking advantage of cheap land associated with Superfund sites. An example is the Old Works Golf Course built on the site of an old copper-smelting facility in Anaconda, Montana. The Anaconda Smelter, a company that extracted metals from ore mined in Butte, Montana, was shut down in 1980 after contaminating more than 1.5 million cubic yards of soil with arsenic, copper, lead, cadmium, and zinc (Superfund 1999). Anaconda residents were wor-

Photos courtesy of Old Works Golf Course.

Above is a stage in the cleanup work done on the site of an old copper-smelting facility in Anaconda, Montana. The site was redeveloped as the Old Works Golf Course, shown below.

ried that their home would turn into a ghost town without the hundreds of smelting jobs and with the severe environmental degradation.

Rather than succumbing to that fate, members of the community partnered with the EPA and the site owner, Atlantic Richfield Company (ARCO), to clean the site and allow redevelopment. The partnership searched for viable solutions that would attract visitors to Anaconda and preserve its historic significance. City Manager Gene Vuckovich suggested making a golf course, which was initially met with skepticism because it had never been done, but eventually his plan was adopted.

The county hired Jack Nicklaus to create a course that successfully incorporated unique historic characteristics from the smelting site, including filling the bunkers with harmless black "slag" that was similar to the by-product left behind by the smelter's furnaces. The Old Works website flaunts that it has "been reborn on the site of Anaconda's historic century old copper smelter. The first course ever built on a federal EPA superfund site." *Golf Digest* praised the Old Works Golf Course as "One of America's 100 Greatest Public Courses" (History 2007).

Who Owns Kermit?

Just as no one washes a rental car, everyone takes care of cars they do own because they are valuable assets. Similarly, until we make the environment an asset, it will not receive the attention it deserves. When landowners benefit from preserving endangered species habitat, they preserve it; when stream owners benefit from improving water flows, they improve aquatic habitat; when fishers own fish or at least a share of the allowable catch, they better manage the fishery; and when producers are held accountable for their emissions, they reduce them.

Unfortunately, it is not always easy to make the environment an asset because doing so requires establishing property rights to environmental resources. A neighbor can hold you accountable for any garbage you dump in her backyard, but it is harder for her to hold you accountable for your carbon emissions. It is relatively easy for a person bitten by your dog to hold you accountable for your dog's actions, but it is more difficult for a livestock owner to hold anyone accountable for wolf predation on his livestock or for brucellosis transmitted to his livestock by wild elk or bison.

Establishing property rights to the environment requires defining and enforcing property rights. Harken back to "those thrilling days of yesteryear," to take a quote from the *Lone Ranger*, to understand this process. On the western frontier, it was not always clear who owned the cattle, land, or water (see Anderson and Hill 2004). Cattlemen defined their rights by branding their cattle and registering their brands, first by brand books published by cattlemen's associations and later by registration with the state. In the absence of a formal process for claiming land in the public domain, cattlemen established customary grazing territories to prevent overgrazing of the commons and hired cowboys to enforce those rights until the invention of barbed wire made property boundaries clear. Water rights were established by diverting water, with priority in drought years given to the earliest diverters. Before those efforts, however, it would have been difficult to imagine how ownership would evolve. But through the imagination and entrepreneurship of people confronted with preventing the tragedy of the commons, property rights did evolve to make the West "not so wild."

Similarly, environmental entrepreneurs, or "enviropreneurs," are taming the environmental frontier. By changing laws to allow leasing and purchase of water for instream flows, water trusts are making stream flows and water quality assets. By establishing shares in a sustainable harvest of fish, anglers are taking the tragedy out of the fisheries commons. And by establishing tradable permits for emitting SO_2 into an airshed or nitrogen and phosphates into a watershed, policymakers have induced people to reduce emissions at a lower cost.

Such success stories seem simple in retrospect, just as do the property rights solutions of the cattlemen. Solving ownership issues for large airsheds (e.g., the global atmosphere), however, are not so simple and may defy market solutions far into the future. If so, we can be sure that applying property rights and markets to the simple problems will leave more collective resources for solving the tough problems.

6 Dancing with Environmentalists

As evidenced by the barrage of greener-than-thou proposals involving slower growth, higher taxes, more regulation, and more centralization, the environmental cause has been captured by people who are uncomfortable with markets and capitalism. Environmentalists bemoan the lack of federal solutions to challenges such as species and habitat preservation, forest management, clean water and air, and global warming. Politicians respond by battling for the regulatory high ground. In fact, the current amount of green regulation in the air could leave everyone gasping for breath. Evidence suggests that a better way to exercise responsible stewardship over natural resources is through local initiatives and markets.

The greener-than-thou movement also includes religious and business leaders who strut their green colors by wrapping themselves in regulatory red tape. Those religious leaders use the pulpit to remind their parishioners of their charge to be stewards of the earth and of the necessary restrictions to correct the failures of humans. And like-minded business leaders call for regulations in the name of a greener planet, knowing that the main benefit to them will be restrictions on competitors.

Despite the strutting, preaching, and lobbying, countervailing movements are on the rise. As discussed in chapter 2, Aldo Leopold embraced the American tradition of private ownership, pined for a stewardship ethic, and advocated compensating landowners who conserve. Leopold may finally be getting his wish via the collaboration of private individuals and groups using voluntary means to preserve land. A proliferation of private land trusts, for example, is protecting evermore land by negotiating with landowners for conservation easements through donations or outright purchases. The *2005 National Land Trust Census Report* showed total acreage conserved by local, state, and national trusts doubling from 2000 to 2005 to reach 37 million acres (Land Trust Alliance 2006). And the number of land trusts has grown to 1,667—a 32 percent increase from 2000 to 2005. This trend "taps deep principles in the American tradition" according to former EPA administrator G. Tracy Mehan (2007, 24).

More reliance on markets to improve environmental quality is not to say that all environmental regulations have been counterproductive. Air and water are cleaner today (see chapter 3), thanks in part to government involvement. Bald eagles have been removed from the endangered species list, though the cause is less from the Endangered Species Act and the ban on DDT and more from the improved habitat on private land. And more than 100 million wilderness acres have been set aside from even use by mountain bikers, let alone loggers.

But have the regulations gone too far? There can be little doubt that they have come with bloated bureaucracies spending billions of taxpayer dollars to achieve environmental gains that could have been realized for much less (see chapter 4). For example, bureaucrats have virtually halted logging in national forests by creating a mass of regulations that are strangling public land managers. Forest Service chief Dale Bosworth (2001, 6) called this "analysis paralysis." The result is that millions of acres are not being husbanded at all, exacerbating the already heavy fuel loads caused by a century of counterproductive fire suppression (Berry 2007). As a result, one spark can cause wildfires costing millions to fight and releasing billions of tons of carbon into the atmosphere. Such nonmanaged lands are also some of the least conducive for wildlife.

Free market environmentalism requires viewing the environment as an asset to be conserved and preserved by private owners rather than considering it a problem to be solved and sustained by govern-

ONLY YOU

CAN PREVENT BUILDING NEXT TO NATIONAL FOREST TINDERBOXES!

Henry Payne: Detroit News/Distributed by United Features Syndicate, Inc.

ment. To do so, we must ask, How can the Forest Service be reformed to reward the prevention of costly forest fires? How can safe harbor agreements turn endangered species into assets? And how can waste areas be transformed into golf courses and mountain biking parks?

To answers these questions and to create more environmental improvements, free market environmentalists must find ways to dance with traditional environmentalists. Conservation writer Jon Christensen (2005) put it well when referring to partisan politics: "It seems at least some in the Grand Old Party have realized they need to learn how to dance with conservationists. . . . Just a word of caution: don't be surprised if your toes get a little tender." The following dance steps offer a starting point for moving beyond seeing the environment as a problem and instead transforming the environment into an asset.

Enviro-Tango

If greener-than-thou environmentalists are more interested in regulations than results, there is not much reason to search for a dance

partner when the music starts. But if it is tangible environmental results that they want, free market environmentalist are ready to party—
and it takes two to tango.

The bumper sticker "Think globally, act locally" provides a starting point. Traditional environmentalists are good at thinking globally,
but their solutions too often call for using large organizations to lobby
for national and transnational regulations.

Free market environmentalism, in contrast, supplies local coop-
erative solutions. To dance with environmentalists will require free
marketers to demonstrate how bottom-up solutions grounded in secure property rights can work around the globe. Recall the story of
the local Bolivian farmers who return their deforested farmland into
cloud forest by creating bee farms, which yield profit from honey
production, create clean water downstream, and save one of the most
fertile yet fragile migratory bird sanctuaries in the world. That program, begun by Natura Bolivia (Asquith 2006), continues to expand
the number of cloud forest acres protected from the chainsaw and
solidify the property rights of the forest landowners by providing them
with beehives and, most recently, barbed wire.

That local action, which has protected a few thousand hectares,
might seem trivial on a global level, but such entrepreneurial actions
not only scale up as they are mimicked by others but are inherently
sustainable because they make both ecological and economic sense.
Natura Bolivia is now partnering with groups in southern Africa and
southeast Asia to see how its approach on the Rio Negra can be applied globally. This type of global replication of local success will syn-
chronize the dance steps of traditional and free market environmentalists.

Although much contemporary environmentalism is intrinsically
antilocalist—preferring public regulation to private action and international treaties to local initiatives—the Center for Conservation Incentives (CCI) is an environmental group that is making an enormous
impact by putting local first. Understanding that landowners want

what is best for their land, CCI (a division of Environmental Defense Fund) is partnering with farmers, ranchers, and private forest owners to protect resources such as endangered wildlife while continuing to keep the land in economically viable production.

That incentive-based management strategy is just getting off the ground. Not long ago, conservation relied on retiring land from agriculture and restoring rare species and their habitats on public lands such as parks and wildlife refuges. And landowners saw a lot more sticks (regulations and lawsuits) than they did carrots (incentives).

Two factors have been key to the successful dance between traditional environmentalists and landowners. First, with nearly three-fourths of the lower forty-eight states privately owned, tackling the nation's most pressing conservation challenges requires active involvement by private landowners. Second, as Leopold predicted, the best means of advancing conservation on private lands is to combine incentives to private landowners for implementing and maintaining conservation measures with a stewardship ethic. In the words of CCI, "to save our natural resources, we need to focus on private property, and voluntary efforts by private landowners . . . . Incentives can accomplish what laws and regulations cannot" (Center for Conservation Incentives 2007, online).

Recall the story of the red-cockaded woodpecker (chapter 2). Despite, or perhaps because of, decades of land regulation under the Endangered Species Act, the red-cockaded woodpecker (RCW) continued to decline. It was not unusual in the mid-1990s to see license plates such as the one on Dougald McCormick's truck that read "IEATRCWS" (McMillan 2005). Why? Because longleaf pine forest owners in the North Carolina sandhills and elsewhere have seen their land use regulated if it poses a threat to the birds. Beginning in 1995, however, North Carolina landowners, with the help of Environmental Defense Fund, helped create the Sandhills Area Land Trust. Attorney Marshall Smith dubbed the area a "Safe Harbor"—reflecting the policy's benefits for both wildlife and landowners. Safe Harbor agreements encourage private landowners to restore and maintain habitat for endangered species without fear of incurring additional regulatory restrictions.

Today, longleaf foresters in seven states have enrolled more than 600,000 acres under Safe Harbor agreements, and woodpecker family groups have increased by at least 10 percent on those lands. And what about McCormick's license plate? Turns out he was one of the first to sign up for Safe Harbor. These days a sandhills landowner is more likely to be seen driving around with a license plate that reads "IGROWRCWS" (McMillan 2005). By growing the endangered red-cockaded woodpecker, McCormick also helps grow longleaf forests and his bottom line.

McCormick's tango with environmentalists goes as follows:

Step 1: Extend your arm to your partner and agree to be true "local yocals." As demonstrated by Bolivian farmers and the Center for Conservation Incentives, landowners want what is best for their land. Local groups can take numerous actions to improve and protect water and air quality, wildlife habitat, and open space. Recall the story of the Wisconsin farmers (chapter 2) who worked with the Fish and Wildlife Service to create the Farming and Conservation Together Committee (FACT). This local group blocked the federal formation of the Aldo Leopold National Wildlife Refuge because they believed like Leopold that land managed by its owner is better cared for. "We really need people to have a chance to point at a map and say 'this is my land, and this is what I know about it,'" explained Jeb Barzen, director of field ecology at the International Crane Foundation and adviser to FACT (Aldo Leopold Foundation 2002). By putting local first, FACT has begun putting into practice its vision of wildlife and agricultural enhancements in central Wisconsin.

Step 2: Get in step with environmental groups focusing on how to "get 'er done." Local land trusts have specific and measurable goals, such as preserving open space, keeping land in farming, or building trails, making it easy to see if they are "getting 'er done." On the other hand, greener-than-thou groups that lobby for more environmental regulations for directing private landowners to provide access or preserve endangered species habitat, or for increases in federal landownership are not prime candidate for dance partners because their measure of success is passing a law, rather than environmental improvements.

Power-to-the-People Polka

In order to "Roll Out the Barrel" with politicians and bureaucrats, governmental self-interest must be channeled to make the environment a political asset rather than an additional dollar in a bureaucratic budget. Politicians and bureaucrats have traditionally approached the environment as a problem in need of regulation. "No One Washes a Rental Car" (chapter 4) is just as much a truism in government as it is in business. Ways must be found to harness the self-interest of politicians and bureaucrats, to give them ownership, and to improve environmental quality.

Fortunately, good models abound. In 2000, Congress created the Valles Caldera National Preserve composed of an 89,000-acre working ranch in New Mexico that had been acquired by the national government. Instead of adding this ranch to the lands of the U.S. Forest Service or the Bureau of Land Management, Congress created a local public trust to manage the property. It mandated that a majority of the board members must be from New Mexico and that board meetings must be held in public and involve the local community. Although the trust currently receives some funding from the federal government, it is tasked with making the preserve self-sufficient through fees for entrance, grazing, and recreation (Yablonski 2004). Valles Caldera represents not only a fresh perspective to existing federal park management but a return to the original vision of national parks as financially self-sufficient. Yellowstone National Park, for example, originally garnered enough revenue to fully cover its costs (see Anderson and Hill 2004).

Another example of the potential for innovative management

based on changing bureaucratic incentives comes from the U.S. Forest Service. In 1998 a group of forestry experts met to discuss issues they faced in managing public lands (for details, see Kemmis 2008). This group proposed the creation of "Region Seven"—a region of public lands made up of experimental forests scattered across the nation. (In 1965 Region Seven was officially absorbed into Regions Eight and Nine, thus eliminating the old Region Seven.) The proposed new Region Seven would include national forest areas from all the other regions that would serve as test areas for experiments with new management regimes. Managers of these forests would be given the freedom to formulate their own environmental objectives and management polices. Although the proposal has yet to be passed into law, it has received serious attention and represents a way of cutting the Gordian knot, which is currently restricting management.

Much also can be learned from the use of fees for public recreation areas. The Recreational Fee Demonstration Program, which was instituted in 1997, authorized 100 percent of the revenue generated from fees to be retained by the managing agency, with 80 percent remaining at the site where they were collected and 20 percent for use agencywide. Those fees have been used to complete deferred maintenance projects on trails, campgrounds, sewer systems, and visitor centers and to conduct research.

Hoping to make the program permanent, land management agencies, including the National Park Service, the Forest Service, the Bureau of Land Management, and the Fish and Wildlife Service, lauded the program in their Fee Demo Program Progress Report to Congress (U.S. Department of the Interior 2004, 7):

> The Fee Demonstration Program represents a major innovation in the management of federal recreation activities. Allowing Fee Demo revenues to be retained by the collecting site has strengthened the incentive to collect fees and has enhanced the ability of federal managers to address high priority needs. . . . [A] permanent recreation fee that encompasses all of the federal land management agencies is

> not only desirable but can be managed in a manner that is sensitive
> to each agency's mission, lands, and recreational opportunities.

As a result, in December 2004, Congress enacted the Recreation En-
hancement Act, giving federal agencies a long-term, multiagency recreation fee program.

Turning to water, although the Clean Water Act has improved
the nation's waters, albeit at a high cost, it could do even more were
it to pay attention to incentives. For example, fertilizers from farms
make their way into major waterways, resulting in marine dead zones
in coastal rivers and bays (see Raloff 2004). This pollution could be
cut significantly if a nutrient trading system similar to that for sulfur
emissions were put in place. (Nutrient trading is the transfer of nutrient reduction credits, specifically those for nitrogen and phosphorus, between buyers that purchase nutrient reduction credits and sell-
ers that offer nutrient credits for sale.) Such trading can reduce the
cause of the environmental concern rather than promote a specific set
of practices.

Fortunately, nutrient trading has already begun. In 2002, the Environmental Protection Agency renewed its support for a market-
based trading system with a proposed water-quality trading policy.
Many regions have developed effluent trading programs. By allowing
dischargers the choice of reducing their own wastewater or paying
others to do so, costs can be reduced and target reductions attained
more rapidly.

North Carolina's Tar-Pamlico trading program serves as an example. After numerous fish kills in the Tar-Pamlico Basin, the state's
Division of Environmental Management created a strategy to reduce
nutrient inputs from around the basin. To avoid tighter permit limits
and reduce the cost of meeting load-reduction requirements, municipal and industrial dischargers formed the Tar-Pamlico Association
(Grippo 2003), which formalized a pioneering trading program between point and nonpoint sources of nutrients in the watershed. In-

stead of individual nitrogen and phosphorus limits for each discharger, the association shares an overall nutrient discharge cap, which
it enforces by allocating discharge limits among its members. The
association's agreement with the state stipulates that, if the collective
annual nutrient caps are exceeded, a fee for every excess kilogram of
nutrients will be placed into a fund that pays farmers to implement
"best management practices" that reduce nutrients. Cap and trade
programs are not always successful, but in this case the Tar-Pamlico
Association has kept nutrient loading well within the set discharge
limits—even with significant economic growth in the basin.

The potential for dancing with greener-than-thou policy makers
is great if we think about harnessing self-interest in the political sector.
Here is how to start the polka:

Step 1: Put your foot forward with policy makers interested in making environmental quality an asset rather than a problem that simply
adds dollars to budgets. Charging fees for parks and forests and
allowing those fees to stay with the resources where they are collected results in enhanced stewardship and better "customer" service. Rewarding private landowners who improve endangered species habitat takes endangered species off their enemies list. Such
changes may fall short of fully private solutions, but a short quick
polka is better than no dance at all.

Step 2: Just as the polka has a chassé to the left and the right, setting
standards and allowing flexibility in meeting those standards needs
to be part of the bureaucratic polka. In the case of nutrient trading,
the chassé to the left allows EPA officials to set standards and the
chassé to the right gives the private sector, with more local knowledge and entrepreneurial drive, the freedom to find effective ways
of achieving those standards. The result is faster and cheaper water
cleanup. Similarly, the proposal to establish a Region Seven of the
Forest Service would give local managers the ability to formulate
environmental objectives and management practices that will meet
those objectives.

Deity Disco

Greener-than-thou preaching has found its way to pulpits across America. The Associated Press reported on November 1, 2007, that religious leaders are finding ecological issues hard to resist. In 1998, mainline Protestant churches lobbied for the passage of the Kyoto Protocol. In 2002, 1,200 religious leaders sent a letter to senators urging energy conservation as a "morally superior" alternative to drilling for oil in Alaska. And in 2006, the Evangelical Climate Initiative (ECI) was launched in what was described by its organizers as a Bible-based response to global warming. The eighty-six prominent signers argued that "this is God's world and any damage that we do to God's world is an offense against God Himself." Moreover, ECI proponents claimed that "most of the climate change problem is human induced" and made predictions that "millions of people could die in this century" (quoted in Acton Institute Press Release 2006).

Religious leaders, according to Michael Barkley (2007) with BeliefNet, should

> remain skeptical of this effort to transform unsound science and policy into a moral crusade. . . . Sound environmental stewardship requires reasoned, prudent judgments about the earth that take into account the best science available and the incentives for human action. Competitive pressures in the marketplace encourage energy conservation by entrepreneurs, especially when the costs of using a resource rise due to its scarcity in a time of great demand. . . . Thus the market helps to see that the good environmental steward is properly rewarded for his efforts without harming the most vulnerable among us.

Religious organizations can and do play a vital role in promoting environmental quality by providing an ethical foundation for stewardship. On the grounds that humans are stewards of God's earth, religion teaches us that we have a responsibility to use natural resources wisely and to leave an environmental heritage for future generations.

This ethical foundation adds to that called for by Leopold; but just as his land ethic requires getting the incentives right, so does a religious ethic calling for stewardship of God's earth. Getting the incentives right requires making individuals accountable for their use of resources and rewarding them for good stewardship. Such an individual accounting system is consistent with most religious teachings. Indeed individual responsibility is at the heart of most religions. Doing the "deity disco" requires finding common ground through environmental ethics and private ownership. Christian economist Peter J. Hill (1988, 25) captures the essence of how Judeo-Christian principles fit into free market environmentalism:

> Establishing private property rights is not the entire answer to our natural resource problems. We also depend upon a high degree of responsibility, tolerance, and mutual understanding. However, since such attitudes have never universally prevailed, moving away from private ownership toward public right will not help the situation; rather it will worsen it.

Hill's point is much the same as Leopold's. Ethics—religious or environmental—condition the way we use our natural capital, but these alone are not enough. Institutions, especially private property rights, are crucial to stewardship.

Where devolution to the individual level may not be efficacious, local communities, as opposed to global initiatives, are the place for action. Consider the New Brunswick, New Jersey–based GreenFaith, an interfaith coalition that works to protect the environment by strengthening people's spiritual ties to nature. As GreenFaith's website attests, "Religious communities are a powerful untapped force for environmental leadership." GreenFaith encourages local religious institutions to act on the link between religion and the earth by publicizing methods of environmental stewardship.

St. Mary's Catholic Church in Colts Neck, New Jersey, is a fine example of a religious community, in partnership with GreenFaith, actively caring for the environment. Father Ed Griswold, of St. Marys said, "As a parish pastor it has been most satisfying to see the effect that our involvement with GreenFaith has had on our community and our awareness of contemporary environmental concerns. As never before we are wrestling with the issues and ways in which we can implement new practices and programs that are both environmentally smart and doable." With GreenFaith's guidance the church has reduced its energy use by 10 percent, participated in voluntary water-pollution testing programs, participated in annual beach cleanups, and partnered with other religious groups to raise environmental awareness. New Jersey governor Jon Corzine gave the Environmental Leader of the Year award to GreenFaith's executive director, Fletcher Harper, for the group's positive influence in the state (GreenFaith).

Doing the Deity Disco requires three basic steps.

Step 1: Embrace informed ethics—secular or nonsecular—as a part of environmental stewardship. We can learn to reduce our effluent and our resource use and to respect the rights of others to environmental quality. Mixing religious ethics with environmental ethics can be a good thing, but we must take care not to follow ethics that result in more environmental degradation. Recycling, for example, can be both ethical and economical, but if more resources are used than are saved in following a recycling ethic, then the result is not environmental stewardship. Curbside recycling, for example, requires that more trucks be used to pick up the same amount of waste. This means more iron ore and coal mining, more steel and rubber manufacturing, more petroleum for fuel, and more air pollution. In the case of curbside recycling environmental costs exceed benefits (see Benjamin 2004).

Step 2: Shine the strobe light directly on the potential for nonsecular community solutions. Religious ethics encourage people to "do unto others," to give unselfishly, and to not be free riders, ethics that can be an integral part of producing fresh air and clean water without resorting to governmental solutions at ever-higher levels. In addition to GreenFaith, the Christian Community Development program is

proving, with more than six hundred organizations in forty states, that grassroots, community-based ministries led by people who have made the community their own are highly effective. The focus, according to the Christian Community Development Association, "is on the community members seeing themselves as the solution to the problem, not some government program or outside group that is going to be their salvation" (www.ccda.org).

Step 3: Don't step on the toes of your partners by resorting to political solutions. Those who embrace economic freedom and efficiency should recognize that ethical values are no less important than material values. Those who embrace religious values should acknowledge that economic freedom and efficiency provide the wherewithal to overcome poverty and thereby to improve environmental quality as discussed in chapter 3. Resorting to political solutions necessitates stepping on other people's toes. Trying to trump ethical values with regulations and subsidies in the name of economic efficiency can mix material and ethical values. Trying to trump economic efficiency and personal freedom with politically imposed ethical values can stifle productivity and create unnecessary conflict between material and ethical values. As in all dances, avoiding the toes of your partner is likely to result in a more enjoyable and productive relationship.

Business Bop

Corporate leaders commonly argue that environmental regulations are too expensive and that they will therefore cripple business enterprises and cost jobs. The standard argument is that there is a trade-off between environmental quality and economic growth. As discussed in chapter 3, however, data suggest that economic growth provides the foundation for environmental improvements, when people who can afford to demand environmental quality do so. Accompanying the argument that environmental regulations cripple business is the argument that governments engage in a "race to the bottom" by weakening regulations to attract business. Again, however, the data do not support the argument. To the contrary, environmental quality can actually become a magnet for business by making a location more attractive for employees (see Fleck and Hanssen 2007).

Such tired arguments are being replaced by new green business strategies. As Adam Smith noted in 1776, "People of the same trade seldom meet together, even for merriment and diversion, but the conversation ends in a conspiracy against the public, or in some contrivance to raise prices" (p. 152). Today he might have added that, "just because they meet under a green banner, the impact on the public and the environment are likely to be the same." Under a greener-than-thou guise, businesses try to sway environmental policy by attempting to set the political agenda and to influence regulations and legislation to protect their interests (see Kamieniecki and Kraft 2007). What appears on the surface to be green, however, may simply be the traditional use of regulation as a ruse to control competition.

The best-known account of greener-than-thou regulation resulting in browner air is the story behind the Clean Air Act amendments of 1977. Environmentalists wanted a reduction in sulfur emissions from coal-fired generating plants in the Midwest on the grounds that they were contributing to acid rain in the Northeast. Because the technology for scrubbing the sulfur dioxide from the emissions was expensive, industry resisted. An alternative proposed by western low-sulfur coal providers was to burn more low-sulfur coal and thus meet the air-quality standards without the expensive scrubbers. Not surprisingly, eastern coal interests, especially those in West Virginia, were opposed. An unholy alliance among environmental groups, industry, and eastern coal miners resulted in amendments that required installing scrubbers on new plants but grandfathered in the old ones. This allowed existing plants to avoid installing the expensive technology, raised the cost to new competitors, kept high-sulfur eastern coal the main source of fuel, and reduced some SO_2 emissions. After the fact, however, it is now clear Americans get dirtier air and higher-cost electricity than had we simply set an emission standard and allowed generators to meet it as they saw fit, in this case by burning low-sulfur western coal.

Law professor Jonathan Adler notes that "green politics is still politics." Given that we spend nearly 2 percent of GDP on pollution control, "seeking regulatory policies that will carve out niche markets or obstruct competition becomes an increasingly profitable investment" (Adler 1996, 26). For this reason, we should not be surprised that the Business Council for a Sustainable Energy Future, a coalition of natural gas, wind, solar, and geothermal energy producers, supports major cuts in greenhouse gas emissions or that electrical utility companies lobby to require the sale of electric cars in major markets such as California and support subsidies for the purchase of electrical cars. This type of greener-than-thou rhetoric may not improve environmental quality, but it likely improves the bottom line for the coalition companies.

One of the most egregious examples of greener-than-thou energy politics is the subsidized production and required sale of ethanol. Such subsidies have encouraged farmers to plant more and more corn on marginal lands that would otherwise be wetlands, forests, or wildlife

habitat. On these lands they use more pesticides, herbicides, and water, which is often pumped from already stressed aquifers. Even some traditional environmentalists are recognizing that ethanol production does more to fill the pockets of farmers and agribusinesses than it does to improve the environment. A report from Environmental Defense Fund points out that corn-based ethanol production can exacerbate water table declines in the Ogallala Aquifer (a vast aquifer encompassing eight states beneath the great plains), with new ethanol plants already taking 2.6 billions gallons a year. The report estimates that 4.6 million acres of lands currently in the Conservation Reserve Program may come back into corn production (see Roberts et al. 2007). In *Sierra*, the magazine of the Sierra Club, Paul Rauber (2007) notes that "corn-based ethanol's contribution to fighting global warming is marginal at best. A debate is raging, in fact, over whether ethanol takes more energy to produce than it provides."

Another greener-than-thou business strategy is referred to as meeting the "double bottom line," meaning that businesses are trying to be profitable and environmentally responsible (or triple bottom line if "social responsibility" is added). Retailers tout their environmental consciousness by giving away energy-saving light bulbs, companies claim to be green because they invest in alternative energy sources, and companies from Google to Coca-Cola to Wal-Mart brag about being sustainable without defining what the term means. Wal-Mart's website states that the company conserves energy to operate its stores, reduces raw materials for construction, and uses renewable materials throughout its stores. Because saving energy and reducing material in construction can reduce costs and therefore increase profits, all of these can make sense for profit-maximizing firms, regardless of their environmental impact.

Ultimately, a business must meet only one bottom line if it is to be in business for the long run and that is the profit test. Unless a business is profitable, it will not survive in a competitive marketplace, especially one that is becoming increasingly global. Hence doing the "business bop" requires adhering to sound business principles rather than to greener-than-thou rhetoric.

There are three steps to the "business bop."

Step 1: Put your right foot directly on the single bottom line. By focusing on profits, businesses can be the perfect engine for environmental sustainability. Whether in pursuit of saving energy, conserving soils, replanting trees, or husbanding nonrenewable energy sources, the private sector has a far better track record than governmental bureaucracies when it comes to economic and environmental efficiency. Conservation Forestry LLC, for example, is an investment organization that aligns private equity with conservation capital for the purpose of acquiring and managing large forest landscapes. The organization emphasizes an acquisition approach in which it purchases the timber cash flows associated with a property and conservation organizations purchase the key conservation amenities through easements and other means. In doing so, the investment fund achieves a superior risk-adjusted return for its investors and leverages the resources of its conservation partners. Similarly, Beartooth Capital invests in ranch real estate to generate strong returns for investors by restoring and protecting ecologically important land. Beartooth acquires undervalued agricultural land and converts it into high-end recreational ranch properties via easements, habitat restoration, and ecologically appropriate limited development. Beartooth also assesses the full array of nondevelopment values embedded in each property, including agricultural, natural resource, conservation, and ecosystem services. Far from sacrificing financial returns to accomplish conservation goals, integrating conservation at the core of Beartooth allows the business to reduce investment risk and generate competitive investment returns (Keith and Palmer 2006). Again, the adage "If it pays, it stays" applies to all business. The business bop focuses on profits from the marketplace rather than profits from politics and as a result is more likely to produce sustainable conservation.

Step 2: Point your left foot in the direction of real environmental entrepreneurs. In the tradition of industrial entrepreneurs such as Cyrus McCormick or Henry Ford, today's environmental entrepreneurs are trying out untested ideas for improving environmental quality in the hope of making a profit. Recall the story of the Remediators from chapter 4. This company uses fungi to clean up contaminated soils. By purchasing dirty sites at a discount, cleaning them up, and selling them at a premium over cleanup costs—dirty dirt becomes an environmental asset. Triton Logging is another example. Triton has discovered how to harvest submerged forests, flooded by reservoirs behind dams. The company has built the world's first deep-water logging machine, appropriately called the Sawfish.™ The machine is a combined unmanned submarine, tree harvester, and tree recoverer. Although the up-front technological costs of creating the Sawfish were substantial, Triton incurs few of the costs of conventional forestry operations. There are no replanting or fire protections costs, no roads to maintain below the watermark, and planning costs are a fraction of those incurred for surface logging. The advantages of underwater logging include safer conditions for loggers (trees float up rather than fall down) and safer areas for those who use reservoirs for recreation. The quantity and potential value of this resource are vast—estimated at 300 million trees worldwide—worth approximately $50 billion (Lucas 2007). As these few examples demonstrate, environmental entrepreneurs have far more potential for improving environmental quality than does greener-than-thou lobbying or posturing.

Step 3: Stick your right arm back into the face of environmental subsidies because most may actually harm the environment, as in the case of corn-based ethanol. Hurricane Katrina provides another example. Katrina was all the more destructive because the federal government tried to fool Mother Nature by subsidizing levy construction and encouraging development in areas with exceedingly high flood risk (see Haddock 2007). Subsidies to deliver electricity to rural areas in the 1920s crowded out wind energy technology that might have continued to improve to this day. (One should also ask how much profitable innovation is being crowded out by such subsidies.) The Conservation Reserve Program, part of the farm program, pays landowners not to crop or graze millions of acres of land. This program may thwart private conservation efforts by land trusts and hunting clubs that want more open space or wildlife habitat.

Conclusion

Command-and-control environmental regulations, which in some cases improved the environment, have had their day. Many of those cases, such as stopping rivers from burning, eliminating smog in cities, protecting the endangered bald eagle, and establishing wilderness areas, are examples of "picking the low-hanging fruit." Legislation regulating point sources of pollution, halting the actual killing of endangered species, and limiting land use to nonmechanized travel in remote areas easily passed Congress because the costs were relatively low and the benefits relatively high.

Going further, however, to pick the higher-hanging fruit, for which the costs are much larger and the benefits more debatable, will require new approaches. Because we live in a rich country, we can all afford to be environmentalists. But simply using greener-than-thou rhetoric, regulations, and religion will not help us harvest the higher fruit.

If the twenty-first century is to be the green century, environmental advocates will have to go beyond seeing the environment as a problem and instead transform it into an asset. Children today are likely to grow up as Generation E—the environmental generation. To move the well-intentioned, but increasingly counterproductive, greener-than-thou approach into truly effective solutions, we must adopt the spirit of enviropreneurs and "get 'er done" free market style—turning Generation E into the "enviropreneur generation."

Bibliographical References

Ackerman, Bruce and William T. Hassler. 1981. *Clean Coal, Dirty Air*. New Haven, CT: Yale University Press.

Acton Institute. 2006. "Evangelical Leaders Exploited by Global Warming—Population Control Lobby." Press release, September 29. Grand Rapids, Michigan.

Adler, Jerry. 2006. "Going Green." *Newsweek*, July 17.

Adler, Jonathan. 1996. "Rent Seeking behind the Green Curtain." *Regulation: The Review of Business and Government* 19, no. 4: 26–34.

Aldo Leopold Foundation. 2002. "Federal Dollars Spur FACT Programs." *Leopold Outlook* Winter. Online at http://aldoleopold.org/about/newsletters/4-1%20Winter%202002/Winter%202002.htm

Anderson, Terry L., and Peter J. Hill. 1996. "Environmental Federalism: Thinking Smaller." *PERC Policy Series*, PS-8. Bozeman, MT: PERC.

Anderson, Terry L., and Peter J. Hill. 2004. *The Not So Wild, Wild West: Property Rights on the Frontier*. Stanford, CA: Stanford University Press.

Anderson, Terry L., and Laura E. Huggins. 2003. *Property Rights: A Practical Guide of Freedom and Prosperity*. Stanford, CA: Hoover Institution Press.

Anderson, Terry L., and Donald R. Leal. 1991. *Free Market Environmentalism*. San Francisco: Pacific Research Institute for Public Policy.

Anderson, Terry L., and Donald Leal. 1997. *Enviro-Capitalists: Doing Good While Doing Well*. Lanham, MD: Rowman and Littlefield.

Anderson, Terry L., and Donald R. Leal. 2001. *Free Market Environmentalism*. Revised ed. New York: Palgrave.

Anderson, Terry L., and Peter J. Hill, eds. 1994. *The Political Economy of the American West*. Lanham, MD: Rowman and Littlefield.

Anderson, Terry L., and Robert McCormick. 2007. "More Inconvenient Truths." *Hoover Digest*, no. 2.

Anderson, Terry L., and Pamela Snyder. 1997. *Water Markets: Priming the Invisible Pump*. Washington, D.C.: Cato Institute.

Annan, Kofi. 2000. "Progress Made in Providing Safe Water Supply and Sanitation for All during the 1990s." *Report of the Secretary-General*. Online at www.un.org/documents/ecosoc/cn17/2000/ecn172000-13.htm (cited June 15, 2006).

Arctic Power. 2005. ANWR Background. Online at www.anwr.org/backgrnd.htm (cited May 29, 2007).

Aristotle. 1984. *Politics*. Translated by Carnes Lord. Chicago: University of Chicago Press.

Asquith, Nigel. 2006. "Bees & Barbed Wire for Water on the Bolivian Frontier." *PERC Reports* 24 (December 4), 3–6.

Associated Press, 2007. "Quoted in Religious Leaders Press Congress for Climate Change Action by Brandon Kiem." *Wired*. November 1. Online at http://blog.wired.com/wiredscience/2007/11/religious-leade.html.

Baillie, Jonathan, Craig Hilton-Taylor, and Simon N. Stuart. 2005. 2004 IUCN Red List of Threatened Species a Global Species Assessment. Online at www.iucn.org/themes/ssc/red_list_2004/2004home.htm (cited June 12, 2006).

Barkey, Michael B. 2001. "The Religious Community's Other Stand on Global Warming." Online at www.beliefnet.com/story/76/story_7610 _1.html.

Barney, Gerald O. 1980. *The Global 2000 Report to the President of the U.S.* New York: Pergamon Publishing.

Becker, Gary. 2007. "An Economist Looks at Global Warming." *Hoover Digest*, no. 2 (spring).

Beer, Jeremy. 2003. "A Greener Shade of Right." *Re: Generation Quarterly* 8, no. 1 (March/April 2003) Online at www.utne.com/cgi-bin/udt/im.display.printable?client.id=utne&story.id=10361 (cited May 18, 2006).

Benjamin, Daniel K. 2003. "Eight Great Myths of Recycling." *PERC Policy Series*, PS-28. Bozeman, MT: PERC.

Berry, Alison. 2007. "Forest Policy Up in Smoke: Fire Suppression in the United States" (white paper available from PERC).

Black, Harvey. 2004. "Imperfect Protection: NEPA at 35 Years." *Environmental Health Perspectives* 112, no. 5 (April 2004). Online at www.ehponline.org/members/2004/112-5/spheres/html (accessed June 11, 2007).

Bookwalter, Genevieve. 2007. "Organic Farmer Sues over Neighbor's Pesticides." *The Santa Cruz Sentinel*, May 10. Online at www.santacruzsentinel.com/archive/2007/May/10/local/stories/04local.htm (cited May 16, 2007).

Bosworth, Dale. 2001. Oversight Hearing on Conflicting Laws and Regulations: Gridlock on the National Forests. Before the Subcommittee on Forests and Forest Health of the Committee onResources, U.S. House of Representatives 107th Congress, Series no.106-76, 6.

Bovard, James. 1994. *Lost Rights: The Destruction of American Liberty*. New York: St. Martin's Press, Inc.

Bovard, James. 1999. "Robbery with an Environmental Badge." *Freedom Daily*, March. Online at www.fff.org/freedom/0399d.asphttp://www.fff.org/freedom/0399d.asp (cited: July 24, 2007).

Boyce, Mike. 2007. Telephone conversation with Katy Hansen, July 30.

Bray, Thomas J. 2005. *Soaring High: New Strategies for Environmental Giving*. Washington, D.C.: Philanthropy Roundtable.

Burnett, H. Sterling. 2006. "Protecting the Environment through the Ownership Society—Part One." NCPA Policy Report No. 282 (January).

Center for Biological Diversity. 2005. "Fort Huachuca Area Lenders Challenged for San Pedro River Harm." April 5, May 19, 2007. Online at www.biologicaldiversity.org/swcbd/PRESS/sanpedro4-5-05.html.

Center for Conservation Incentives. 2007. Why Private Lands? Online at www.environmentaldefense.org/page.cfm?tagID=442.

CEQ Review of NEPA. 2002. Summary of Public Comment. Chapter 1, 222. Online at www.nepa.gov/ntf/catreport/ccg-app-6.pdf.

Chavez, Karen. 2006. "Saving Face: Rock Climbers Group Raises $250,000 to Buy Laurel Knob." *Citizen-Times.com* (accessed August 14, 2007). Online at www.mountainlandsusa.com/articles/LaurelKnobSaving.htm.

Christensen, Jon. 2005. "White House to Greens: We Should Totally Do This Again Some Time." *Grist*, September 2. Online at www.grist.org/com ments/soapbox/2005/09/02/christensen-conf/.

Christensen, Jon. 2006. "Unlikely Partners Create Plan to Save Ocean Habitat Along with Fishing." *New York Times*. August 8. Online at http://72.14.253.104/search?q=cache:sVFrzBD5bMEJ:www.esm.ucsb.edu/academics/courses/200/Readings/christensen.doc+Gordon+Fox+preserve+fisheries+off+the+coast+of+central+California+lawsuit&hl=en&ct=clnk&cd=1&gl=us.

Citizens against Government Waste. 2006. Government Pig Book Summary. Online at www.cagw.org/site/PageServer?pagename=reports_pigbook2006 (cited June 13, 2006).

Cizik, Richard. 2007. Quoted in "12 Ideas for the Planet." *Newsweek*, April 16, p. 92.

"Come Rain or Come Shine; Weather Risk." 2007. *The Economist* 382, no. 8515 (February 10).

Coulter, Michael. 2005. "House Task Force Hears Testimony on Improving Decades-Old Environmental Law." *Environment News* (Heartland Institute) August 2005. Online at www.heartland.org/PrinterFriendly.cfm?theType=artId&theID=17567 (accessed 4/18/2007).

Cromwell, Brian A. 1989. "Capital Subsidies and the Infrastructure Crisis: Evidence from the Local Mass-Transit Industry." Federal Reserve Bank of Cleveland. Q II. 11–21.

Dennis, William C. (forthcoming). *The Environment for Liberty: Liberty and the Place of Man.*

Ehrlich, Paul. 1968. *The Population Bomb.* New York: Sierra Club–Ballantine Books.

Ehrlich, Paul R., and John P. Holdren. 1971. "Impact of Population Growth." *Science* 171: 1212–17.

Eilperin, Juliet, and Michael Fletcher. 2007. "Bush Proposed Talks on Warming." *Washington Post*, May 31.

Environment Agency. 2007. Summary—General Quality Assessment for Rivers in England and Wales, 2005. Online at www.environment-agency.gov.uk/yourenv/eff/1190084/water/213902/river_qual/gqa2000/186186/?version=1&lang=_e (cited June 28, 2007).

Environmental Defense Fund. McDonald's Partnership Marks 10th anniversary. Online at www.environmentaldefense.org/article.cfm?contentID=981&campaign= (cited September 7, 2006).

Environmental Protection Agency. 2003. Draft Report on the Environment. Online at www.epa.gov/indicators/roe/http://www.epa.gov/indicators/roe/ (cited June 18, 2006).

Environmental Protection Agency. 2007a. Air Quality and Emissions: Progress Continues in 2006. Online at www.epa.gov/airtrends/econ-emissions.html (cited June 4, 2007).

Environmental Protection Agency. 2007b. PM Research. Online at www.iucn.org/themes/ssc/red_list_2004/factsandfigures_EN.htm (cited May, 31 2007).

Environmental Protection Agency. 2007c. Great Lakes Binational Toxics Strategy: 2006 Progress Report. Online at www.epa.gov/glnpo/bns/reports/2006glbtsprogressreport.pdf (cited June 27, 2007).

Environmental Protection Agency. 2007d. Polychlorinated Biphenyls (PCBs). Online at www.epa.gov/pcb/ (cited July 24, 2007).

Environmental Protection Agency. 2007e. DDE. Online at www.epa.gov/ttn/atw/hlthef/dde.html (cited July 24, 2007).

Environmental Protection Agency. 2007f. Hexachlorobenzene. Online at www.epa.gov/ttn/atw/hlthef/hexa-ben.html (cited July 24, 2007).

Evenson, R. E., and D. Gollin. 2003. "Assessing the Impact of the Green Revolution, 1960 to 2000." *Science* 300, no. 5620: 758–62.

Fishman, Charles. 2006. How Many Light Bulbs Does It Take to Change the World? One. And You're Looking at It. Online at www.fastcompany.com/subscr/108/open_lightbulbs.html (cited September 1, 2006).

Fleck, Robert K, and F. Andrew Hanssen. 2007. "Do Profits Promote Pollution? The Myth of the Environmental Race to the Bottom." *PERC Policy Series*, PS-41. Bozeman, MT: PERC.

Flippen, J. Brooks. 2000. *Nixon and the Environment*. Albuquerque: University of New Mexico Press.

Food and Agricultural Organization of the United Nations. 2006. *Global Forest Resources Assessment 2005*. Rome, Italy: FAO. Online at www.fao.org/forestry/foris/webview/forestry2/index.jsp?siteId =101&sitetreeId=1191&langId=1&geoId=0 (cited July 7, 2006).

Freedom House. 2005. *Freedom in the World 2005: The Annual Survey of Political Rights and Civil Liberties*. Oxford: Rowman & Littlefield.

Fretwell, Holly Lippke. 1999. "Paying to Play: The Fee Demonstration Program." *PERC Policy Series*, PS-17. Bozeman, MT: PERC. Online at www.perc.org/perc.php?id=393.

Fretwell, Holly Lippke. 2004. "Public Land Management." In *2004 Index of Environmental Indicators*. San Francisco, CA: Pacific Research Institute.

Fretwell, Holly Lippke. Forthcoming. *Minding the Federal Estate*. Lanham, MD: Lexington Press.

Freyfolge, Eric T. 1999. "Aldo Leopold on Private Land." In *The Essential Aldo Leopold: Quotations and Commentaries*, ed. Curt Meine and Richard L. Knight. Madison: University of Wisconsin Press.

Freyfogle, Eric T. 2006. *Why Conservation Is Failing and How It Can Regain Ground*. New Haven, CT: Yale University Press.

Friederici, Peter. 2006. "Is the Big Cat Back?" *Defenders Magazine* 81, no. 2.

Friedman, Thomas L. 2007. "The Power of Green." *New York Times*, April 15.

Gawell, Karl, and Alyssa Kagel. 2006. "GEA Update." *Geothermal Energy Association*, March 30.

Goklany, Indur M. 2007. *The Improving State of the World*. Washington, D.C.: Cato Institute.

Gore, Al. 2006. *An Inconvenient Truth*. New York: Rodale Press.

"Green America: Waking Up and Catching Up." 2007. *The Economist*, January 25, pp. 22–24.

GreenFaith. 2007. Members in Action. Online at www.greenfaith.org/members/stmarys.html.

"Greening Bush: An Unusual, but Sensible, Suggestion for the Homecoming President." 2005. *The Economist*, March 5, p. 34.

Grewell, Bishop. 2002. "Farming for the Future: Agriculture's Next Generation." *PERC Policy Series*, PS-26. Bozeman, MT: PERC.

Grippo, April. 2003. "Nutrient Trading: A Bridge over Troubled Water." *Stormwater: The Journal for Surface Water Quality Professionals*. January/February. Online at www.forester.net/sw_0301_nutrient.html.

Grist. 2006. About *Grist*: Where We Reveal Our True Selves. Online at www.grist.org/about/ (cited September 1, 2006).

Haddock, David D. 2007. "Warning: Army Corps of Engineers Project Ahead." *PERC Reports* 3, no. 25 (Fall): 26–29.

Hardin, Garrett. 1968. "The Tragedy of the Commons." *Science* 162: 1243–48.

Hays, Samuel P. 1959. *Conservation and The Gospel of Efficiency: The Progressive Conservation Movement, 1890–1920*. Cambridge, MA: Harvard University Press.

Hayward, Steven F., and Amy Kaleita. 2007. *Index of Leading Environmental Indicators*. San Francisco, CA, Pacific Research Institute. Online at http://liberty.pacificresearch.org/docLib/20070418_07EnvIndex.pdf (cited June 7, 2007).

Hess, Karl Jr. 1997. "Wild Success." *ReasonOnline* (accessed August 14, 2007). Online at www.reason.com/news/show/30401.html

Hill, P. J. 1988. "Markets and Morality." *PERC Viewpoints* (January/February). Bozeman, MT: PERC.

"History." *Old Works Golf Course.* Online at www.oldworks.org/ history.aspx (accessed: July 24, 2007).

"House Budget Proposal a Grand Slam for National Parks." 2007. *National Parks Conservation Association's Park Lines.* June. Online at www.npca.org/ take_action/park_lines/national_priority0607.html (accessed: July 16, 2007).

Huey, John. 1998. "Sam Walton: Wal-Mart Brought Low Prices to Small Cities, but Its Creator Also Changed the Way Big Business Is Run." *Time,* December 7. Online at www.time.com/time/time100/builder/profile/ walton.html (cited August 23, 2006).

Hurst, James Willard. 1956. "Law and Conditions of Freedom in the Nineteenth Century United States." *American Political Science Review* 51, no. 3: 832–33.

Intergovernmental Panel on Climate Change (IPCC). 2001. *Climate Change 2001: The Scientific Basis.* Cambridge: Cambridge University Press. Online at www.grida.no/climate/ipcc_tar/wg1/index.htm (cited June 27, 2007).

Jum'ah, Abdallah S. 2006. "The Impact of Upstream Technological Advances on Future Oil Supply" President and Chief Executive officer, Saudi Aramco, address to OPEC, Vienna, Austria, September 13, 2006.

Kamieniecki, Sheldon, and Michael E. Kraft, eds. 2007. *Business and Environmental Policy: Corporate Interests in the American Political System.* Cambridge, MA: MIT Press.

Kanhema, Tawanda. 2006. "$54 Million Jumbo Tusks Recovered." *The Herald-Zimbabwe.* October 22, p. 4.

Kauffman, Jason. 2007. "Gov. Otter Signs Wood River Legacy Project into Law." *Idaho Mountain Express,* April 2. Online at www.mtexpress.com/ vu_breaking_story.php?bid=3466? (cited June 14, 2007).

Keith, Robert, and Carl Palmer. 2006. "Beartooth Capital Partners: Mixing Business and Conservation." *PERC Reports* 24, no. 4 (December): 14.

Kemmis, Daniel. 2008. "Institutional Reforms for Public Lands?" In *Accounting for Mother Nature: Changing Demands for Her Bounty,* ed. Terry L. Anderson, Laura E. Huggins, and Thomas Michael Power. Stanford, CA: Stanford University Press.

LaMonica, Martin. 2006. Investors See Green in Clean Tech. July 20, 2005.CNET Networks Inc.

Land Trust Alliance. 2006. *2005 National Land Trust Census Report*. Washington, DC.

Larwanou, M., M. Abdoulaye, and C. Reij. 2006. "Etude de la Regénération Naturelle Assistée dans la Région de Zinder (Niger): Une Première Exploration d'un Phénomène Spectaculaire." Prepared for the United States Agency for International Development (USAID). Online at www.cilss.bf/doc/etude_zinder.pdf (cited July 18, 2007).

Leal, Donald. 2006. "Saving Fisheries with Free Markets." *Milken Institute Review* 8, no. 1 (Santa Monica, CA, the Milken Institute).

Leal, Donald, and Bishop Grewell. 1999. *Hunting for Habitat*. Bozeman, MT: PERC.

Lee, Dwight R. 2005. "To Drill or Not to Drill: Let the Environmentalists Decide." In *Re-Thinking Green: Alternatives to Environmental Bureaucracy*, ed. Robert Higgs and Carl P. Close. Oakland, CA: Independent Institute.

Leopold, Aldo. [1923] 1991. "A Criticism of the Booster Spirit." In *River of the Mother of God and Other Essays by Aldo Leopold*. Madison: University of Wisconsin Press.

Leopold, Aldo. [1928] 1991. "The Home Builder Conserves." In *River of the Mother of God and Other Essays by Aldo Leopold*. Madison: University of Wisconsin Press.

Leopold, Aldo. [1934] 1991. "Conservation Economics." In *River of the Mother of God and Other Essays by Aldo Leopold*. Madison: University of Wisconsin Press. Originally published in *Journal of Forestry*, 32 (May 1, 1934): 537–44.

Leopold, Aldo. [1935] 1991. "Land Pathology." In *River of the Mother of God and Other Essays by Aldo Leopold*. Madison: University of Wisconsin Press.

Leopold Aldo. [1939] 1991. "The Farmer as a Conservationist." In *River of the Mother of God and Other Essays by Aldo Leopold*. Madison: University of Wisconsin Press.

Leopold, Aldo. 1966. *A Sand County Almanac: With Other Essays on Conservation from Round River.* New York: Oxford University Press.

Libecap, Gary D. 2005. "Rescuing Water Markets: Lessons from Owens Valley." *PERC Policy Series*, PS-33. Bozeman, MT: PERC.

Libecap, Gary D. 2007. Owens *Valley Revisited: A Reassessment of the West's First Great Water Transfer.* Stanford, CA: Stanford University Press.

Lieberman, Ben. 2004. "Air Pollution Cut in Half, EPA Announces." *Environment News* (November). Online at www.heartland.org/Article.cfm ?artId=15891 (accessed 4 June 2007).

Lomborg, Bjorn. 2001. *The Skeptical Environmentalist.* New York: Cambridge University Press.

Lovelock, James. 2006. *The Revenge of Gaia: Earth's Climate Crisis and the Fate of Humanity.* New York: Basic Books.

Lucas, James. 2007. "Water Logged." *PERC Reports* 25, no. 4 (Winter): 24–27.

Lueck, Dean, and Jeffrey A. Michael. 2003. "Preemptive Habitat Destruction under the Endangered Species Act." *Journal of Law and Economics* 46, no. 1: 27–60.

McMillan, Margaret. 2003. "The Preacher and the Toad." *Conservation Incentives* (November): 5.

McMillan, Margaret. 2005. Safe Harbor's First Decade: Helping Landowners Help Endangered Wildlife. Online at http://environmentaldefense.org/ article.cfm?contentID=4666.

Meadows, Donella H., Dennis L. Meadows, Jorgen Randers, and William W. Brehens III. 1972. *The Limits to Growth.* New York: Universe Books.

Mehan, Tracy. 2007. "Land of the Free: Private Solutions Propel the Conservation Boom." *American Conservative*, April 23: 23–25.

Meine, Curt, and Richard L. Knight, eds. 1999. *The Essential Aldo Leopold: Quotations and Commentaries.* Madison: University of Wisconsin Press.

Meiners, Roger E., and Andrew P. Morris, eds. 2000. *The Common Law and the Environment: Rethinking the Statutory Basis for Modern Environmental Law.* Lanham, MD: Rowman & Littlefield.

Meiners, Roger E., and Lea-Rachel Kosnik. 2003. "Restoring Harmony in the Klamath Basin." *PERC Policy Series*, PS-27. Bozeman, MT: PERC.

Miller, Char. 2001. *Gifford Pinchot and the Making of Modern Environmentalism.* Washington, D.C.: Island Press.

Miller, James E. 2007. "Evolution of the Field of Wildlife Damage Management in the United States and Future Challenges." *Human-Wildlife Conflicts* 1, no. 1: 13–20.

Miller, Roger LeRoy, Daniel K. Benjamin, and Douglass C. North. 2005. *The Economics of Public Issues.* 14th ed. Boston: Pearson Addison-Wesley.

Minnis, Natalie, and Kerry Mackenzie, eds. 2004. *Insight Guides: Chile.* 4th ed. Singapore: APA Publications; GmbH & Co. Verlag KG.

Morris, Edmund. 2001. *Theodore Rex.* New York: Random House, Inc.

Murray, John Q. 2005. "If Congress Can't Solve Gordian Knot, Planning Rule Won't Either." *Clark Fork Chronicle* 2, no. 13 (April 1). Online at www.clarkforkchronicle.com/20050401/bolle-jwt-20050401.htm (accessed May 18, 2007).

Myers, Norman. 1979. *The Sinking Ark: A New Look at the Problem of Disappearing Species.* Oxford: Pergamon Press.

National Agricultural Statistics Service (NASS). 2007. Statistics by Subject: Crops and Plants. In *QuickStats* database. Washington, D.C.: NASS, a department of the United States Department of Agriculture. Online at www.nass.usda.gov/QuickStats/indexbysubject.jsp?Text1= &site-ASS_MAIN&select=Select+a+State&Pass_name=&Pass_group= Crops+%26+Plants&Pass_subgroup=Field+Crops (cited June 27, 2007).

New York City Department of Environmental Protection. 2003. *2003 New York Harbor Water Quality Report: Overview of Long-Term Trends.* Online at http://home2.nyc.gov/html/dep/hwqs/html/over.html (cited June 7, 2007).

Nistler, Carolyn. 2007. "Seeing Spots: The Return of the Jaguar." *PERC Reports* 25, no 4 (Winter): 12–15.

Northern Jaguar Project. 2006. Online at www.northernjaguarproject.org (cited July 18, 2007).

Norton, Gail. 2003. "Conservancy from the Grass Roots." *Washington Post.* June 7, A23.

Nugent, Sam. 2006. "Mushrooms Meet Brownfields: A Market for Fungal Remediation." *PERC Reports* 24, no. 4 (December). Online at http://news.com.com/Investors+see+green+in+clean+tech/2100-1008_3-5796707.html.

Office of Technology Assessment. 1988. "Are We Cleaning Up? 10 Superfund Case Studies—Special Report." *Congressman Report.* OTA-ITE-392. June. Washington, D.C.: U.S. Government Printing Office.

O'Riordan, Timothy J. 1988. "The Politics of Sustainability." In *Sustainable Environmental Management*, ed. R. K. Turner. Boulder, CO: Westview Press.

Perkowitz, Bob, and Lisa Renstrom. 2006. "Wake Up and Smell the Progress." *Grist Magazine*, August 10. Online at www.gristmill.grist.org/story/2006/8/10/12426/4827 (cited August 23, 2006).

Polgreen, Lydia. 2007. "In Niger, Trees and Crops Turn Back the Desert." *New York Times*, Feb. 11, Section 1, p. 1.

Postel, Sandra L., Gretchen C. Daily, and Paul R. Ehrlich. 1996. "Human Appropriation of Renewable Fresh Water." *Science* n.s., no. 271: 785–88.

Pound, Edward. 1997. "Costly Outhouses Monuments to Red Tape. *USA Today*, December 15. Online at www.jldr.com/oh1mill.html.

"Problems in Paradise. In Tarnished Jewels: The Case of Reforming the Park Service." *Different Drummer.* Online at www.ti.org/npsprobs1.html (accessed: July 24, 2007).

Raloff, Janet. 2004. "Dead Waters: Massive Oxygen-Starved Zones Are Developing along the World's Coasts." *Science News* 165, no. 23 (June 5): 360.

"Rating the Parks." 1997. *Consumer Reports*, June 10–17, p. 12.

Rauber, Paul. 2007. "Detroit's Phony Ethanol Solution." *Sierra*, January/ February. Online at www.sierraclub.org/sierra/200701/decoder.asp.

Rauch, Jonathan. 2003. "Will Frankenfood Save The Planet?" *Atlantic Monthly*, 292(3): 103–8.

Reiger, John F. 2001. *American Sportsmen and the Origins of Conservation.* 3d ed. Corvallis: Oregon University Press.

Riedl, Brad. 2005. Park-Barrel Spending Is a Corrupting Practice in Need of Reform. February 9, 2005. Online at cbsnews.com/stories/2006/02/09/ opinion/main/300712.shtml

Ring, Ray. 2005. "Strange Bedfellows Make a Grazing Deal in Idaho." *High Country News*, October 3.

Roach, John. 2004. "By 2050 Warming to Doom Million Species, Study Says." *National Geographic News*, 12 July. Online at news.nationalgeographic.com/news/2004/01/0107_040107_extinction.html (cited May 24, 2007).

Robinson, Michael J. 2006. "Habitat for Jaguars in New Mexico." *Arizona Game & Fish*. Online at www.gf.state.az.us/w_c/es/documents/ NEWMEXICOJAGUARHABITATREPORT.pdf (cited July, 25 2007).

Rothberg, Robert. 2002. "Mugabe Ratchets Up the Misery in Zimbabwe." *Christian Science Monitor*, December 19. Online at www.ksg.harvard.edu/ news/opeds/2002/rotberg_mugabe_csm_121902.htm (cited May 25, 2007).

Runte, Alfred. 1990. *Trains of Discovery*. Niwot, CO: Robert Rinehart.

Samuelson, Robert J. 2006. "Wal-Mart's a Diversion." *Newsweek* 148, no. 10 (September 4).

Scarborough, Brandon, and Hertha L. Lund. 2007. *Saving Our Streams: Harnessing Water Markets*. Bozeman, MT: PERC.

Schoenbrod, David. 2000. "Protecting the Environment in the Spirit of the Common Law." In *The Common Law and the Environment: Rethinking the Statutory Basis for Modern Environmental Law*, ed. Roger E. Meiners and Andrew P. Morriss. Lanham, MD: Rowman and Littlefield.

Schwartz, Joel. 2003. *No Way Back: Why Air Pollution Will Continue to Decline*. Washington, D.C: AEI Press

Schwartz, Joel. 2004. "Finding Better Ways to Achieve Cleaner Air." American Enterprise Institute for Public Policy Research. Sept. 1, 2004. Online at www.aei.org/publications/filter.,pubID.21225/pub_detail.asp (accessed May 21, 2007).

Schwartz, Joel. 2008. "Cleaning the Air." *PERC Reports* 26, no. 1 (Spring).

Serrill, Michael S. 1997. "Ghosts of the Forests." *Time*, special issue, October 27.

Simmons, Randy T., and Kim Frost. 2004. *Accounting for Species: The True Costs of the Endangered Species Act*. Bozeman, MT: PERC. Online at www.perc.org/perc.php?id=393.

Skari, Tala. 2002. "Look Out Below: Tourism and Global Warming Are Destabilizing Europe's Biggest Glaciers, with Potentially Disastrous Results." *Time International* 160, no. 3: 42.

Smith, Adam. 1999. *The Wealth of Nations*. Revised ed. Penguin Classics. London: Penguin Books.

Sourcewatch. 2006. Environmental Defense and Free Market Environmentalism. Online at www.sourcewatch.org/index.php?title=
Environmental_Defense_and_Free_Market_Environmentalism (cited August 24, 2006).

Sowell, Thomas. 2002. *A Conflict of Visions: Ideological Origins of Political Struggles*. New York: Basic Books.

Stark, Mike. 2006. "Agreement Ends Sheep Grazing in Area Rife with Wolves, Bears." *Billings Gazette*. March 16. Online at www.billingsgazette.net/articles/2006/03/16/news/state/30-grazing-area.txt (accessed on July 12, 2007).

Stern, Nicholas. 2006. *The Economics of Climate Change: The Stern Review*. Cambridge: Cambridge University Press.

Stiglitz, Joseph E. 1993. *Economics*. New York: W.W. Norton.

Stone, Brad. 2006. "The Color of Money." *Newsweek*, November 13. Online at www.msnbc.msn.com/id/15549205/site/newsweek/.

Stroup, Richard L. 1996. "Superfund: The Shortcut That Failed." *PERC*

Policy Series, PS-5. Bozeman, MT: PERC. Online at www.perc.org/ perc.php?id=393.

Stroup, Richard and Sandra Goodman. 1992. "Property Rights, Environmental Resources and the Future." *Harvard Journal of Law and Public Policy* 15, no. 3 (Spring): 427–54.

Superfund Redevelopment Program. 1999. "Old Works/East Anaconda Smelter Case Study." *U.S. Environmental Protection Agency*. January. Online at www.epa.gov/superfund/programs/recycle/success/casestud/anaccsi.htm (accessed July 24, 2007).

Underhill, William. 2006. "Here's Dr. Doom: A Founding Father of Environmentalism Has Embraced Fatalism—and the Public Loves It." *Newsweek International*, April 24.

United States Department of Agriculture. 2008. "Agricultural Productivity in the United States," Online at www.ers.usda.gov/Data/AgProductivity/

Utah Geological Survey. 2007. "Gasoline Questions and Answers." State of Utah. Online at http://geology.utah.gov/sep/energy_efficiency/gasoline/ gas_q&a.htm.

Viscusi, W. Kip, and James T. Hamilton. 1999. "Are Risk Regulators Rational? Evidence from Hazardous Waste Cleanup Decisions." *American Economic Review*, 89 (4): 1010–27.

Watts, Myles. 2006. "Federal Grazing Contracts and Environmental Incentives." *American Economic Review.* Submitted 2006.

Wigley, T. M. L. 1998. "The Kyoto Protocol: CO2, CH4 and Climate Implications." *Geophysical Research Letters* 25(13): 2285–88.

World Bank. 1994. *World Development Report 1994.* New York: Oxford University Press. Online at www-wds.worldbank.org/external/ default/main?pagePK=64193027&piPK=64187937&theSitePK =523679&menuPK=64187510&searchMenuPK=64187511&siteName= WDS&entityID=000009265_3970716142907 (cited July 9, 2006).

World Conservation Union. 2004. *The IUCN Red List of Threatened Species: A Global Species Assessment*, ed. Jonathan E.M. Baillie, Craig Hilton-Taylor, and Simon N. Stuart. Online at www.iucn.org/themes/ssc/ red_list_2004/GSA_book/Red_List_2004_book.pdf (cited June 4, 2007).

Worldwatch Institute. 1998. *Accelerating Demand for Land, Wood, and Paper Pushing World's Forests to the Brink.* Online at www.worldwatch.org/node/1620 (cited May 31, 2007).

Yandle, Bruce. 1997. *Common Sense and Common Law for the Environment: Creating Wealth in Hummingbird Economies.* Lanham, MD: Rowman & Littlefield.

Yandle, Bruce, Maya Vijayaraghavan and Madhusudan Bhattarai. 2004. "Income and the Race to the Top." In *You Have to Admit It's Getting Better*, ed. Terry L. Anderson. Stanford, CA: Hoover Institution Press.

Illustration
Acknowledgments

Page 82: Bumper sticker slogan. Used courtesy of Montana Land Reliance. www.mtlandreliance.org

Page 89: Photograph ©Del Leu. All rights reserved. Used with the permission of photographer. Photo of traffic congestion at the entrance to Zion National Park, Utah, appeared in *E/The Environmental Magazine*, Volume XI, No. 5, September/October 2000. www.DelsJourney.com/news/news_01-06-15_p2.htm

Page 91: Photograph ©Peter Franzen. All rights reserved. Used with the permission of photographer. www.franzen-online.com

Page 93: Photos courtesy of the Old Works Golf Course, Anaconda, Montana. www.oldworks.org

Page 99: Henry Payne cartoon, November 5, 2007, ©Detroit News/ Distributed by United Features Syndicate, Inc. All rights reserved. Used with permission.

Page 110: Mick Stevens, *New Yorker* cartoon. All rights reserved. Used with the permission of CartoonBank.com; July 29, 2002, image no. 52394.

Page 114: Ed Fischer cartoon. All rights reserved. Used with the permission of Cartoon Stock, Ltd.; catalogue reference: efin287. www.CartoonStock.com

About the Authors

Terry L. Anderson, the John and Jean DeNault Senior Fellow at the Hoover Institution, is the executive director of PERC (the Property and Environment Research Center) and professor emeritus at Montana State University. Anderson is the author or editor of more than thirty books, including *The Not So Wild, Wild West: Property Rights on the Frontier* (Stanford University Press, 2004), co-authored with Peter J. Hill, which was awarded the 2005 Sir Antony Fisher International Memorial Award; *Property Rights: Cooperation, Conflict, and Law*, coedited with Fred S. McChesney (Princeton University Press, 2003); and *You Have to Admit It's Getting Better: From Economic Prosperity to Environmental Quality* (Hoover Institution Press, 2004).

Laura E. Huggins is a research fellow at the Hoover Institution and director of publications at PERC—a think tank in Bozeman, Montana, that focuses on market solutions to environmental problems. Huggins is the author, along with Anderson, of *Property Rights: A Practical Guide to Freedom and Prosperity* (Hoover Institution Press, 2003) and is the editor with Anderson and Thomas Power of, *Accounting for Mother Nature: Changing Demands for Her Bounty* (Stanford University Press, 2008). She has also edited *Population Puzzle: Boom or Bust?* (Hoover Institution Press, 2004) and *Drug War Deadlock: The Policy Battle Continues* (Hoover Institution Press, 2005).

Index

BOOKS OF RELATED INTEREST FROM THE HOOVER INSTITUTION PRESS

You Have to Admit It's Getting Better:
From Economic Prosperity to Environmental Quality
edited by Terry L. Anderson

Property Rights:
A Practical Guide to Freedom and Prosperity
by Terry L. Anderson and Laura E. Huggins

Agriculture and the Environment:
Searching for Greener Pastures
edited by Terry L. Anderson and Bruce Yandle

Political Environmentalism:
Going behind the Green Curtain
edited by Terry L. Anderson

Breaking the Environmental Policy Gridlock
edited by Terry L. Anderson